THEORY OF EDUCATIONAL ADMINISTRATION

Global Education Series-15

THEORY OF EDUCATIONAL ADMINISTRATION

B.M. Sharma

Commonwealth

Theory of Educational Administration

Edition : **2026**

ISBN 81-7169-449-7

Published by
COMMONWEALTH PUBLISHERS (P) LTD.
4831/24, Govind Lane,
Ansari Road, Darya Ganj,
New Delhi - 110002
Ph. : 23272541, 23242541
e-mail : commonwealthpublishers2016@gmail.com

Distributed by :
ARJUN PUBLISHING HOUSE
4831/24, Govind Lane,
Ansari Road, Darya Ganj,
New Delhi - 110002
Ph. : 23272541, 23242541
e-mail : arjunbooks2001@gmail.com

Laser Typesetting by :
Dimple Computers
Delhi

Printed at :
Roshan Digital Printers
Delhi

Preface

In the field of education in India emphasis has been laid especially in the last decade or so on the quality and excellence of educational administration at all levels. In the selection of teachers for the tertiary level, academic excellence in a particular discipline was preferred rather than pedagogical skills and an understanding of the psychology of students. Further efforts were not made to help teachers to develop their teaching skills on scientific lines. In consonance with these viewpoints, the need to bring out instructional and reference materials that could be profitably used by teachers at the tertiary level is indeed, most urgent.

In this book, denotes the broad field of educational administration at the tertiary level and focuses on instructional strategies and theoretical approach. This book aims to provide the necessary professional knowledge and guide the teachers to develop the required skills to make their administrative talent effective. The administrative strategies described and suggested for adoption are based on sound psychological, sociological and philosophical foundations.

This book is an indepth study about the developmental aspects of educational administration.

Editor

Preface

Contents

1
Theory and Motivation in School

Most readers with some teaching experience will be able to recognize the above and add to the list. Motivation is a powerful explanatory concept that would appear to be deeply embedded in the thinking and folk wisdom of members of the teaching profession. All teachers and most pupils will have a working conception of motivation. Motivation is the thing that explains why one person does better at a task than another even though both appear to have equal ability.

Motivation is the thing that leads to one person working long and hard at a task while another stops at the first excuse. Motivation is the thing that enables one pupil to work with the minimum of direction and guidance from the teacher, while another child has to be constantly monitored and directed. However, push at the concept of motivation a little, ask a few awkward questions concerning its more precise nature and, often, its explanatory power seems to melt away. Notice that the paragraph above offered not so much definitions of motivation itself, but definitions of the things that motivation supposedly does. They tell us much more about the differences between those who apparently have a lot of it, and those who do not, than they do about the entity itself.

If the concept of motivation is to fulfill its apparent promise regarding its power to explain differences in educational success and failure, then it is necessary to begin to build up a working model of motivation itself. It is necessary to have an understanding of the concept that not only informs us as to the consequences of having different levels or types of motivation, but also explains why such differences might occur and how they operate. Furthermore, if this understanding is to have educational consequences, in the sense of providing teachers with practically useful conceptual tools, then it must provide an analysis of motivation that is relevant to classroom processes.

These points have not escaped the attention of psychologists to date and there have been several attempts to conceptualize motivation, to develop theoretical accounts of its development and operation and to devise programmatic interventions from these theories.

This chapter looks at one of these conceptualizations, that developed by Weiner and his various associates. This model draws on one of social psychology's currently dominant theoretical systems, attribution theory. Attribution theory attempts to develop a model of the ways in which people will ordinarily make judgments concerning the causes of events. Attribution theorists regard these judgments as significant as, in common with other 'cognitive' approaches to the study of human bebaviour it is an individual's understanding of a situation, rather than the situation itself, that is held to determine the ways it which they react. From the early work of Heider onwards, attribution theorists have held that people's beliefs concerning the causes of events are critical in determining the understanding that they have of those events.

A simple example will serve to illustrate the point. Two pupils have both attempted a maths test at school. Each does badly on he test in comparison to other members of the class. Let us assume that each child is concerned about his performance and asks himself why it came about. One child decides that his performance is the result of his idleness over the last couple of weeks. He had not attended to the lessons that the test was related to, he had not done his homework. The second child decides that his performance was the result of a basic lack of mathematical ability. He is simply the kind of person who does not do well at maths tests. Attribution theorists will go on to claim that these two differing explanations of what was, objectively, the same level of performance, make the performance levels quite different in terms of their subjective import for the pupils concerned. The first pupil is likely to conclude that future improvements are possible. If he attends to future lessons, if he does his homework, there is no need for him to perform as poorly again. The second pupil is likely to conclude that extra work and effort will be a waste of time. If you can't do it you can't do it and that is that. To put it another way — the first child's failure provides a motivationally useful 'kick-in-the-pants' while the second's proves to be debilitating.

The contribution of Weiner

'Attribution theory' is in many respects a poor descriptive term. As generally understood by present day social psychologists, the term refers not so much to a single articulated theory, but rather to a somewhat loose collection of research studies and attempts to explain the data thus produced. Some social psychologists have more or less abandoned the term and refer instead to the psychology of ordinary explanations. These approaches all share one basic concern, however, which is an examination of the ways in which people explain or attempt to explain events that have happened to them or to others about whom they are concerned to some notable degree.

The approach taken by the attribution theorists has been classified into two broad categories, each of which is capable of further subdivision. The first group is referred to as 'theories of attribution'. Here the concern is with the ways in which individuals make decisions concerning the causes of events that they wish to explain. Given that an event has taken place, just how does a person decide what caused it to happen, and why might one individual arrive at a different conclusion from another? The second category, of 'attributional theories', concerns attempts to explain the consequences of a decision to attribute an event to a particular cause. As will be clear from a re-examination of the example given above, concerning two pupils' reactions to the results of a maths test, any attempt to use attribution theory to explain reactions to success and failure within the school context will need to incorporate elements of both categories.

Initially we will need to know whether attributing instances of success and failure to different causes seems to have any bearing on performance, then we will need to know why, and to what extent, apparently similar circumstances might be explained differently.

Classifying the causes of success and failure

Weiner's approach to beginning to untangle this was to

assume that whereas the list of causes to which an instance of success or failure *might* be attributed is potentially longer than the number of people making the attributions, there may well be certain features of causes that are critical in their consequences and that would reappear in a number of apparently differently described causes. If this were to be the case, then it ought to be possible to classify causes for success and failure along dimensions that are related to these key features, and then to assume that all causes that share a location on the resulting classification system will be essentially similar in their effects.

Full details of the reasoning that has guided the development of the classificatory systems can be seen elsewhere. The 1979 statement of theory by Weiner is the one that currently guides most work in the area. In the 1979 publication Weiner identified four dimensions that seemed to account for the majority of attributions made by individuals in a variety of situations. It ought, however, to be pointed out that it is still the case that much of the evidence for this claim is drawn from laboratory studies rather than from those carried out in the field, in our case the school classroom. There is now evidence to show that attributions made under classroom conditions are very varied and may possibly require a different category system.

The first is the internality dimension. Causes of success and failure can vary according to the degree to which they can be seen to reside within the actor or within the situation. A success seen to be determined by the ability or effort of the actor would be an internally caused success, whereas one seen to be caused by the ease of the take or the actions of others would be externally caused.

In the majority of cases there will the agreement among individuals as to where any cause ought to be located. Ability would be seen by most members of our culture as being internal, that such consensus is not always apparent. Luck, for example, may be seen by some as residing in the situation whereas others might see themselves as being typically lucky people. The crucial point, however, is the location of a cause in each case. As we shall see later, internal causes and external causes are held to have different consequences.

The second dimension that Weiner refers to is stability. A stable cause of success and failure will be one that remains the same and has a constant effect over a period of time. Unstable causes, on the other hand, are subject to change. Ability and the difficulty of the task are typically seen as examples of stable causes of success and failure, while effort and luck are typical examples of unstable causes. Again it is important to realize that an apparently similar cause, that is, one given the same descriptive label by two or more people, might be seen by them to have different properties that will lead it to have different places on a dimension. Effort, for instance, would seem to be seen by most people as an unstable cause. No doubt we can all recall instances where the effort we put into a particular task has varied considerably overtime. For some people, however, effort will be seen to be a stable cause of success and failure. They would regard themselves as being typically lazy or typically industrious. Ability, as we shall see later, can be seen in quite different ways by children at different stages of development.

The third dimension is that of controllability. Some causes of success and failure can be varied at will, others cannot. Ability is generally regarded as being uncontrollable. Either you have it or you don't. Effort, on the other hand, is often regarded as being a controllable cause.

Finally, Weiner's fourth dimension is globality. A global cause is one that has far-reaching effects, whereas a specific one is limited in respect to the range of events that it will influence. Ability is a cause that can be seen to vary along the globaility dimension. In some cases, or to some people, a lack of ability might be seen to have global consequences. One believes oneself to be hopeless at everything. On other occasions, or when a different person is making the judgment, the ability judged to be lacking is seen to be specific to one particular task. To return briefly to the example given above, the pupil who attributed the failure to a lack of ability might assume that this deficiency was peculiar to maths. In this case the cause of the failure would have been judged to be specific. Alternatively, the pupil might have decided that the lack of ability was global in which case it would be seen to apply to most areas of endeavour.

In this most recent statement of the complete theory, Weiner expresses these dimensions somewhat differently, describing them in terms of three main dimensions: locus; constancy; and responsibility. While not having any great impact on the implications of the theory this classification is clearer and more doubtless come to supersede it. The 1979 formulation, however, is, for the moment at least, the account of the theory that the majority of published work will make reference to.

The antecedents and consequences of attributions

Attribution theorists have concerned themselves with

theories of attribution and attributional theories. In respect to the present discussion, these tow major lines of enquiry reduce to a concern with the factors that lead an individual to attribute an instance of success or failure to any one particular cause, or combination of causes, rather than to any other, and to a concern with the consequences of having done just that. To the practising teacher, both are of equal concern. In order to emphasize the importance of the claims that are being made here, we will begin by looking in greater detail at the claimed consequences of attributing an instance of success or failure to any particular cause.

The consequences of attributions for success and failure

Weiner has identified two major types of consequences both of which he sees as having important implications for the motivational reactions of the individual concerned. The first of these concerns the expectations for the future that an individual might have, while the second relates to that individual's affective reaction to the success or failure.

The effects on expectations are the more clearly understood, indeed Weiner goes as far as to claim that the relationship described by attributional theory has the status of a fundamental law of psychology. Weiner's concern is with the effect that attributions will have on *expectancy shifts*, rather than on the expectancy itself. The major determinant of the expectancy would seem to be the outcome of the event itself. In other works, following success we are likely to expect more success and following failure, more failure. However, the *degree* to which this is true will depend upon the attribution made to explain the success or failure.

The relevant dimension is constancy. The more

constant the cause of a success or failure is assumed to be, over time or place, the greater will be the degree to which we will expect more of the same. For example, an instance of failure, attributed to a lack of effort, will produce a relatively low expectation for future failure. After all, we have to do to avoid a repeated failure is to work harder. An apparently similar failure, attributed to a more constant cause, such as ability would give rise to a more confirmed expectation of future failure. The research supporting this claim need not be explored in any detail here.

A moment's reflection will lead to the conclusion that there is a clear advantage, from the motivational point of view, to adopting a certain pattern, or style of attributions for success and failure. The pupil who consistently attributes his or her successes to stable causes, but their failures to unstable causes, will progressively come to hold higher and higher expectations for future success. Every success will confirm the view that more success is on the way, while failures will not carry a similar implication. At the other extreme, there is a clear motivational disadvantage to adopting a style that leads to stable attributions for failure, but unstable ones for success. For such an individual each failure will bring with it doom laden predictions for continuing lack of success, while successes, when they do come, will be seen as only temporary respites.

The claimed existence of these differ, *typical* responses to success and failure lies at the heart of the attributional approach to the study and understanding of motivation in the school context. Pupils are seen as responding not just to instances of success and failure themselves, but to their own interpretation of them.

The second major type of consequence, identified by Weiner, is concerned with the affective responses to success and failure. Most people would react to failure with a negative affect, say shame, and to success with positive affect, say pride. Weiner's initial conception was a straightforward one. To the degree that an outcome was attributed to an internal cause the affect associated with it would be heightened. To the degree that it was associated with an external cause the associated affect would be reduced. So, everyone will be likely to feel proud following success, but those who believe that the success was caused by something about themselves will experience the greatest pride. Similarly, failure makes us all feel bad, but never more so than when we are convinced that the failure was the result of something to do with us. On the other hand, of course, if we can equally confidently attribute a failure to something to do with the situation our feelings of shame will be considerably reduced.

This argument has a convincing ring to it, but it has been shown to be only part of the story. A study by Weiner, Russell and Lerman demonstrated what, with the benefit of hindsight, ought to have been obvious beforehand. That is, that while pride and same may be the major affective reactions to success and failure they are not the only ones. The study is important for two reasons. Firstly, it reveals a more complex pattern of relationships between attributions and affect than the one initially suggested. Secondly, and in the long term more significantly, it has important implications for research methods. In this study, Weiner and colleagues allowed the participants to respond freely with descriptions of their affective states over a number of different situations. Previously the concern had been to demonstrate that the logically derived relationships held up in practice, an approach that frequently excluded the discovery of other relationships.

The present position seems to be that a variety of affects will follow success and failure, and that the particular attribution made will influence the one that is experienced. For instance, guilt is likely to follow if a failure is attributed to a personally controllable cause whereas gratitude will follow if a success is seen to be due to factors personally controllable by others.

The link between attributions and affect has been taken up in a somewhat different manner by Covington and his colleagues. Covington's researches have led him to the conclusion that affect ought to be seen not so much as a consequence of attributions but rather as one of their major determinants.

The link with affect for Weiner is, nevertheless, still very important. If different individuals do develop consistent ways of attributing success and failure then they are likely to come to hold, increasingly, expectations for either success or failure, and to have certain afffects more clearly associated with those outcomes. The individual who regularly attributes success to a stable and internal cause, can be assumed to be much more likely to anticipate success confidently and to relish that success than does the individual who consistently attributes success to unstable causes. Attributing failure to a stable, internal cause is likely to generate very negative attitudes towards achievement situations.

The antecedents of attributions for success and failure

What has been outlined above shows how attributions influence reactions to success and failure. In order to understand why different individuals experience varying reactions to success and failure it is necessary to outline in a similar manner the factors held to influence in process of making these attributions.

Bar-Tal has presented an outline of the processes which influence the attribution process. He argues that antecedents of attributions for success and failure can be divided into two major categories, each of which can be further subdivided. The first major category is the pupil's own dispositions and history, while the second concerns the information currently available to him or her.

The major subdivision carries with it some possibly important implications for the teacher. To the extent that personal dispositions play a part in determining the pattern of attributions produced by any one individual, we may be obliged to conclude that any resulting motivational patterns will be difficult, if not impossible, for the teacher to influence. To the degree that the information available to the pupil from the current context is the major influence, however, teacher influence becomes more feasible.

For some significant degree of teacher control to be a realistic proposition some important conditions need to be met. First, that pupils' attributions are indeed influenced by the current context. Secondly, that the relevant aspects of this context are potentially controllable by the teacher. Thirdly, that the potentially controllable is put under *actual* control. This final assumption is an important one that is often overlooked in discussions of the educational implications of attribution theory. Rogers has argued that attribution theorists need to concern themselves much more with educational issues defined in the way that educationists themselves would define them, if their work is to have any impact on educational practice. In respect to present concerns, this would seem to reduce to first attempting to communicate the concern of attribution theory to the teaching profession and second, ensuring that research attends to the practicalities of manipulating the context of real classrooms.

Personal dispositions clearly do play an important part in determining the nature of attributions for success and failure. One of the first concerns of attribution theorists, wishing to establish an account of motivational behaviour in attributional terms, was to demonstrate links between patterns of attributions and established measures of achievement motivation or the need for achievement have shown that those high in the need for achievement will tend to attribute success to effort or ability and failure to lack of effort. Those low in the need for achievement will have no clear attributional pattern for success but will tend to attribute failure to a lack of ability. Results such as these are essential as far as development of the theory is concerned for they allow the attributionists to demonstrate links with the mass of research that has been generated by the need for achievement literature.

Following closely from this in conceptual terms, was the concern to demonstrate links between the pattern of attributions that an individual now demonstrates, and that individual's history of success and failure. A fuller introductory account of this work can be seen elsewhere. The major conclusion is that individuals are likely to attribute expected outcomes to stable causes and unexpected outcomes to unstable causes. From this general principle it clearly follows that those with a history of success are more likely to attribute further successes to a stable. It will also be recalled that Weiner argues that attributions to stable factors generate more confident expectations that the outcome will be repeated. In this way a beneficent cycle is set up—success breeds success. On the other hand a history of failures makes success unexpected, leading to an attribution to an unstable cause in turn making further success seem relatively unlikely. This can also be seen to be part of a cyclic process only this time the effects are vicious rather than beneficent. Expected and unexpected failure, determined by the degree to which past failure can be considered to be characteristic, gives rise to similar and complementary effects. One of the challenges that attribution theory provides for the teacher concerns attempts to break these cycles when to do so would be to the pupil's advantage.

Various demographic factors, such as race and socio-economic class have been shown to be related to attributional patterns. Those in ethnic minority groups and from lower social-class groups tend to demonstrate attributional patterns that would be disadvantageous educationally.

A further demographic factor that is currently generating considerable research interest is the sex of a pupil. Rogers has reviewed some of the literature on this. A number of studies have demonstrated the existence of sex differences in the attribution of success and failure. Broadly these studies indicate that girls and women across a number of different tasks and situations are more likely to attribute failures to lack of ability and less likely to recognize the presence of ability as a cause of their own successes. As with race and class effects, those who tend to do less well in the educational system also seem to have the less adaptive attributional patterns.

The brief discussion of sex-differences in attributional style above serves to lead us into a discussion of the ways in which the present situation might influence the attributional patterns of pupils. The sex of the pupil is, of course, something that the teacher does not influence. It is fixed prior to the commencement of school and the study by Lochel, referred to above, shows that attributional patterns also become associated with gender before compulsory schooling starts. However, while teachers cannot influence the sex of their pupils they can, and apparently do, react to it. These reactions will form part of the information that is available to a pupil at any one time and might therefore influence the ways in which attributions are formed.

Studies by Dweck and her colleagues, which are now widely cited in the literature examining the different performance patterns of boys and girls at school, are indicative of a link between patterns of teacher-pupil interaction, and the patterns of attributions that those pupils come to demonstrate.

Dweck's research demonstrated two things. Firstly that patterns of interaction between teachers and young pupils varied according to the sex of the pupil. Secondly, that such patterns of interaction could influence attributions for success and failure. In essence the research showed that in the early stages of schooling teachers would appear to be creating a more favourable environment for girls in that the female pupils received fewer instances of criticism relating to non-academic aspects of their school behaviour. However, this lack of general criticism helps to establish a situation where the criticism that a young girl pupil does receive is highly likely to be criticism directed at the actual quality of her work. Such concentrated criticism is thought to have an influence different from the criticism that the typical boy pupil would receive. When criticized for aspects of his work, the boy will perceive this against a background of a relatively high level of criticism for a whole range of activity. The girl therefore more likely to take the teacher's criticism of her work as an indicator of a lack of ability. The boy is more likely to see it as something else, perhaps just another sign of the bias that teachers seem to have against boys.

A second piece of research in the same paper demonstrates that both boys and girls would be influenced, in terms of the attributions that they made, by the pattern of feedback directed at them. Those that received feedback similar to that shown to be typical for girls in classrooms were more likely to attribute failure to a lack of ability. Those that received more generalized criticism were more likely to attribute failure to a lack of effort or to the hostility of the judge. This latter finding strongly suggests that it is the patterns of interaction established between pupils of each sex and their teachers that are important for the determination of attributional styles and not the sex of the pupils *per se*.

Research of this kind is important, as it whose the ways in which an attributional approach to the analysis of classroom practices can be beneficial. The paradox uncovered by the Dweck research is this. While girls in the early years of their schooling would appear to be developing within an environment that is more favourable than that experienced by the boys, this same environment is actually encouraging girls to assume that failure implies a lack of ability. Remember from our earlier discussion of the consequences of attributions that one likely outcome of this would be girls coming to believe that they are less likely to be successful in subject areas that are believed to be difficult and therefore to demand high levels of ability.

Interactions with teachers then are likely to be an important source of information for the pupil that will be used by the pupil in the process of making decisions about the causes of instances of success and failure. Bar-Tal catalogues a variety of ways in which teachers will influence the attributions of their pupils.

The first of these in verbal appeals and covers the kind of pattern that Dweck unearthed. Different types of verbal feedback will have different effects. There is also evidence to suggest that the instructions given to pupils regarding a task will have an influence on attributions. Kukla has demonstrated that subjects will respond differently on a task dependent upon their level of achievement motivation and degree to which they have bee led to believe that the task is one that requires ability and/or effort to successfully complete. Research currently being undertaken by Rogers that will be briefly discussed later indicates other ways in which the means of instruction used by the teacher might influence attributions.

Bar-Tal's third category of teacher behaviour is referred to as reinforcements. Of greatest concern here is the degree to which a teacher uses cooperative or competitive reward systems. Expensive research is now available concerning the effects of cooperative and competitive forms of instruction and Nicholls have produced evidence showing that attributions will be influenced by these different reward systems. In particular it is claimed that cooperative reward systems are more likely to produce attributional patterns that are associated with a relatively high level of intrinsic motivation. That is, pupils that are less fearful of failure, and more willing to engage in tasks without the teacher having to continually dangle carrots or wield sticks.

The fourth category of teacher behaviour is verbal feedback. Evidence from the classroom seems to be very limited here, but Bar-Tal cites laboratory based studies to show how comments following success or failure can influence attributions. For example, there would seem to be a tendency for people to assume that someone who receives some degree of criticism after success must have a high level of ability. Rogers in a similar vein, demonstrates the somewhat patronizing attributions that are made by boys with respect to the successes and failures of girls.

Finally Bar-Tal points out that teachers can quite deliberately influence attributions. Work by Dweck, Andrews and Debus and DeCharms shows that it is possible to systematically influence patterns of attributions by setting up an attribution retaining programme.

The work by attribution theorists has demonstrated that attributional patterns and motivational patterns seem to be related to each other. Attributions are held partially, at least, to determine motivational patterns by influencing a pupil's expectations for success and failure and the affective reactions that he or she has toward those events. In turn, it is possible to determine the factors that influence the makings of attributions. What is most encouraging from the teacher's point of view is that many of these factors seem to be located within the classroom and are potentially under the control of the educational system, if not the individual teacher.

Developmental factors

One element that is not given sufficient attention in many accounts of the attribution process in schools, including some of Weiner's own accounts, is the effects of development. Rogers outlines some of the research that indicates general age-related changes in the ways in which children understand causal relationships and the values that they put upon different causes of success and failure. More recently, however, research more sharply focused on developmental changes within the school context has been producing results that have some very important implications for an analysis of the development of motivational style over the schooling period. One of the leading workers in this area has been Nicholls and it is his research that will be focused on here.

As has been made clear above, attribution theorists believe that instances of success or failure influence the motivation of individuals through the ways in which those individuals interpret success and failure events. It is clearly the case, therefore, hat a success attributed to ability will be likely to have different motivational implications from one attributed to luck, or to effort. If this is actually to be the case then it must follow that each individual has concepts of ability, effort, task difficulty and all the other possible causes of success and failure, that are clearly differentiated from each other. One of the more significant claims made by Nicholls is that young children frequently will not have fully differentiated from each other concepts such as ability and effort. Further, he goes on to own light, important implications for the operation of motivation in educational settings. His case will be illustrated here by outlining parts of the developmental process that he has identified.

There are two key aspects of development according to Nicholls. The first of these concerns the development of the concept of difficulty. Nicholls identifies three levels here. During the first, the egocentric stage, the child assumes that those things which he or she expects to be able to succeed on are easy and those where they do not are difficult. No reference is made to the successes of others or to any other aspects of the task.

In the second stage, the objective level, difficult task are seen to be ones that have the appearance of complexity. A jigsaw puzzle, for example, that has many small pieces would be judged to be more difficult than one that has a few large pieces. Adults, of course, will also use such a mode of judgment. The point that Nicholls is making is that younger children will not be able to operate at any more sophisticated levels.

The final stage, the normative conception of difficulty, comes when the child begins to define task difficulty in terms of the proportion of people attempting it that would gain success. An easy task is now seen to be one on which most people would be successful, and a difficult one would be a task at which most would fail. These judgments are clearly independent of your own assessment of your own chances of success. Whereas at the first level it was, by definition, impossible to expect to fail an easy task, by the third level this is no longer so. The key point that emerges from this analysis is that by the final stage the degree of difficulty attributed to tasks undertaken has implications for the self-concept.

Central to this self-concept will be assessments of levels of effort and ability. These are also subject to developmental change. Four stages are identified by

Nicholls representing a development from a position where effort, outcome and ability are hardly distinguished at all through finally to the adult view of ability as a capacity. At this final level ability is seen to be a relatively fixed aspect of a person's nature that will set an ultimate limit upon what they can achieve, irrespective of the amount of effort they may deemed to be impossible to exceed it on a regular basis. A run of good luck may produce some exceptional results in some circumstances, but this does not last.

Taken together, these two developmental patterns have some important implications for the ways in which a pupil will perceive failure at various tasks. As the child moves towards the normative view of difficulty, he will become increasingly concerned with how others have performed. This growing concern with the performance for others also leads the child to be increasingly concerned with the reasons for his own performance, *relative* to that of others. This relative perspective heightens the importance of internal causes.

At the same time the child becomes increasingly concerned to avoid including that failure is caused by lack of ability, while also becoming more likely to conclude that his prospects are poor if he does attribute failure to a lack of ability. In an argument that develops increasingly close links with the work of Covington, Nicholls states that the older child will be increasingly concerned to avoid failures that might imply a lack of ability. One clear way of doing this is to not try very hard, thereby providing a built-in explanation for failure. Alternatively the pupil could select only very difficult tasks or very easy tasks were failure is highly unlikely to occur. These various strategies are not well suited to the maximization of the child's school progress.

This analysis by Nicholas, even in the very abbreviated from provided here, presents some intriguing possibilities. One of these is that the oft noted decline in intrinsic motivation as the child progresses from primary to secondary school has more to do with the development of the concepts of ability than it does with the differing modes of teaching and organization employed at the two levels of the school system.

Prospects for the future of an attributional approach to motivation

Work on attribution theory as related to schooling continues apace. From what we know already it is clear that there is a link between the motivational patterns that a child will display and the way in which that child attributes success and failure. Furthermore there are links between these attributional patterns and various school-related experiences including actions of the teacher and the degree to which school work is set up on cooperative or competitive lines. Overriding this, it is now clear that aspects of the child's cognitive development during the years of schooling will have an important impact on the implications of the explanations of success and failure that the child devises.

Work in the future is likely to concentrate on three main areas. The first of these will be the development of motivational style. Nicholls' collection reveals a large number of research avenues that seem ripe for further exploration. The second will be the further development of attribution retaining programmes. The third will be the increased examination of the types of attributions made by children across a variety of different organizational frameworks.

This latter work is very much in its infancy at present. However, it does seem to show promise. Little has shown that when allowed to express their attributions for success and failure in their own words, schoolchildren in the 5-14 age range will use a much wider variety of causes than those typically covered by attributional research. Rogers is beginning the task of examining the ways in which these wider and more complex categories of causes are employed across a variety of different kinds of school work. For example, early results seem to imply that children are more likely to attribute success or failure in maths to ability when the maths work is presented to them in the form of a test than when presented in the form of work completed individually at the child's own pace. If such effects can be reliably and systematically demonstrated, then is ought to become possible for attribution theory to provide the basis for a system of examining various schemes of work with a view to identifying their likely motivational impact.

Above all else, attribution theory provides teachers with a conceptual framework with which they can begin to analyze their own classroom practices and the reactions to those practices of their pupils. At the outset of this chapter it is stated that if we are to be able to realize the apparent thus were not oriented to the details of the passage they read. Interestingly, however, conceptual learning was as high in the ND condition as in the NCD condition and children in these two conditions had higher conceptual learning than those in the CD condition. The argument that pressure and control undermine the active procedures of integration of information was thus supported by these findings.

Some of the most compelling results of this study

occurred, however, as the one-week follow-up session. We were interested in how the environments for learning would affect the retention of the information children learned. Examination of the difference between the amount of rote information recalled at the follow-up relative to the relative to the initial learning session revealed that children in the CD condition lost the most information between our sessions. We would argue that this indicates that information learned because of instrumental goals and pressure is poorly maintained because once the outcome is achieved i.e., the test taken or the reward attained, there is no longer any reason to further process the information. We have previously referred to this as the 'core dump' phenomenon whereby information force fed into the system is dumped following completion of the program.

The fact that conceptual learning was as good in the non-controlling-directed condition as compared to the non-directed condition was surprising. It indicates, however, that children do pick up an integrate information encountered in their environments without any direction to do so. As Montessori would argue, we often fail to capitalize on this natural tendency to learn believing that children need always to be directed. What accounts for this natural learning? Ryan, *el al.* examined natural or 'spontaneous' learning in a study with college students. They found that, when spontaneous learning occurred, it was a function of the extent to which students were interested in the material and felt no pressure or 'ego-involvement' while learning. Thus, increasing spontaneous learning may involve decreasing pressure and control.

The Grolink and Ryan study, thus, provided evidence that learning conditions relevant to autonomy can have consequences for the quality of learning and retention of information as well as for the emotional experience of learning. However, recent research has shown that the quality of learning outcomes is not solely a function of the environment but also of the motivational orientation of the learner. In order to examine how individual differences in children's motivational stance in school affects learning, children in the Grolnick and Ryan study completed the Self-Regulation Questionnaire.

Children's self-determination in school, as indexed by the SDI, was then related to emotions and learning outcomes. Because of their more active approach to learning, more self-determined learners were expected to exhibit better integration of information resulting in higher conceptual learning and retention of information relative to more externally oriented learners. Similarly, more self-determined learners were expected to find our learning materials more interesting and experience less pressure in our learning session than their less self-determined counterparts.

Analyses investigating relations between children's self-determination and learning generally supported these hypotheses. Across learning conditions, more self-determined children evidenced higher conceptual learning and the lower feelings of pressure and tension while reading. In addition, the more self-determined learners lost less information between our initial and follow-up sessions relative to those who were less self-determined. Thus, not only to immediate conditions for learning influence the change the information will be integrated, children's orientations to learning may facilitate or undermine integrative processes as well.

These orientations may be a function of long-term

experience with autonomy-supportive versus controlling home and school environments.

Ryan and Grolnick in a subsequent project further explored individual differences in motivational orientations and learning outcomes in a developmental study of third through sixth graders. Children at each grade level were asked to read the fifth grade level materials used in the previous study within a spontaneous learning context. Thus, children were asked to read the materials but not told that any kind of learning assessment would follow. Their emotional reactions and rote and conceptual learning were then assessed as in Grolnick and Ryan's study. Interestingly, the results differed strongly by grade. For fifth graders, the results were virtually identical to those in the previous study, i.e., more self-determined styles in children were associated with higher conceptual learning, lower experienced pressure and better retention of information relative to lower self-determined styles. However, for third and fourth grade children the results were the opposite. Although none of the children displayed high conceptual scores or described very low levels of pressure, self-determined styles were negatively associated with these indices.

These results can be interpreted in terms of the importance of optimal challenge or level of difficulty in motivation. We suggest that children are self-determined to integrate only information or regulations that are congruent with their internal structures and abilities. The material was not optimally challenging for our younger subjects and so only external orientations could push the children to learn. Thus, in providing learning contexts facilitative of autonomy or self-determination, it is crucial to be sure that information presented is at or just above the current ability level of the student. Material too difficult or too easy will undermine self determination and motivation.

The issue of self-determination and optimal challenge for learning have also been explored in research by Danner and Lonky. Using the approach of cognitive evaluation theory and Piaget's equilibration model, they tested the hypotheses that children would be most intrinsically motivated to assimilate material just above their current level of ability; and that extrinsic inducements would interfere with this natural propensity to seek optimal challenges. They studied an elementary school population engaged with conceptual sorting tasks and obtained results supporting these propositions. Their findings fit with those above in suggesting that motivational principles are crucial to the production of quality learning.

When considering the kinds of learning that educators value and hope to facilitate, it is clear that the issue of autonomy and optimal challenge are of great importance. In order to conceptualize this, we consider the outcomes of two contrasting models of learning: integration and accretion. Integration, a process of development, is evident when information is acted upon and transformed by the learner into a form where it can be meaningfully integrated into existing, internal structures. It therefore requires autonomous energy on the part of the learner. Because such learning is integrated with past knowledge and skills, it is more likely to be maintained over time and transferred to new contexts. Accretive learning, on the other hand, can be force-fed to the child because it involves no energy on the part of the learner. In this model, the prescriptions and motivations of learning are the teacher's rather than the learner's. Accretive learning involves knowledge acquired in a passive, rote manner and is therefore less likely to be maintained or generalized. Because the ultimate goals of teaching involve learning that is integrated, maintained, and generalizable, providing a context for learning which supports autonomy must be a goal for education.

2

Education and Modernisation

Due to Science and technology the pace of progress has been amazingly accelerated during the twentieth century. Now man has left his foot-prints on the face of the moon. He is travelling from place to place faster with meteoric speed. He has almost conquered the time and space. Industrialisation has given a material culture unprecedented. Agriculture has been revolutionised and the biological, mechanical and chemical processes have increased the yield beyond imagination. The most distinctive feature of a modern society, in contrast with a traditional one, is its adoption of a science-based technology". In all fields production has increased spectacularly with the utilisation of all modern means, materials and methods. This applied technology has also many other significant effects on and implications for social and cultural life and it involves fundamental, social and cultural changes which are broadly described as "modernisation".

Essentially, modernisation denotes a dynamic process, a powerful movement from traditional quasi-traditional order to certain desired types of technology and the resultant changes in the social structure, value orientation, motivation, achievements and aspirations. It implies change in the value system and involves the substitution of old images and structures with new ones. The modernised countries can not be imitated blindly. One country's model cannot be adopted indiscriminately by another. A country must retain its entity and should not sacrifice its originality in craze for modernity. The ecology of modernisation presupposes certain infrastructure like the wholesome political ideology, its effective operation, viable national economy, functionally literate population, skilled manpower, dynamic value system, high motivation, etc. The explosion of knowledge, rapid social change, need for rapid advance and so on are responsible for modernisation.

India was considered to be one of the advanced nations of the world. Before the advent of Britishers, India was educationally and culturally more advanced than most of the Western countries. The attainment of Independence created high aspirations and strong motivations for launching a revolution which would be epoch-making and spear-headed to undo the harm done by the British system through countries, make up the deficiencies and bring about a takeoff in all aspects of her national life.

There has been unprecedented explosion of knowledge during the last few decades. In a traditional society the quantum of knowledge is very limited gradually increases so that one of the main aims of education i.e., preservation and maintenance of existing culture, is achieved. But in a modern society, the quantum of knowledge is too vast and the rate of its growth is too fast. One of the important tasks of education is to keep pace with this progress of knowledge and teach the student to acquire such knowledge "how" rather than "what". So process is found more important than product and critical as well as creative powers are encouraged.

In India, as in other countries where similar conditions prevail, this would require, among other things, a new approach to the objectives and methods of education and changes in the training of teachers. Unless they are trained in new ways of teaching and learning, the students in schools and colleges will not be able to receive the type of education needed for the new society. It was rightly considered desirable to revamp, revise and overhaul the educational system which was ineffective and even irrelevant in the changed circumstances. The most outstanding measures taken by Free India are in respect to provision of huge, funds, opening of thousands of educational institutions, appointment of teachers in large numbers and so on.

Another feature of a modern society is the dynamic process of social change. In a traditional society the process of social change is very slow and conservatism of the educational system does a little or no harm. However, in a modern society change is so rapid that the educational system has to keep itself abreast with the latest developments. Therefore, it is imperative to adopt a dynamic policy and infrastructure of education which can continually renovate itself. Otherwise, it will not only hamper progress, but also tend to create a lag between national aspirations and realities. So education is to be a dynamic process, not only for imparting knowledge as a finished material but also to generate interests and curiosity, inculcate attitudes and values and teach essential skills for independent study and judgment. This is necessary for enabling students to be competent citizens of the future for initiating as well as adapting with the drastic social changes.

An important aspect of modernisation is a new

equilibrium to be reached and maintained. Any change in the society upsets various factors and thereby brings about many difficulties and problems. The old equilibrium gives way to a new one. Thus to change the society for setting up a new social order means in its trail a large number of problems—social, economic, cultural and political which demand immediate solution. Half-hearted solutions of faltering steps to solve these problems cannot bring about improvement, rather setback and harmful effects. That is why, a new equilibrium is to be set up with full knowledge and implications of modernisation. For this, political leadership is significant but education has to play an important role and technological preparedness is also necessary. Education works as the potential instrument of modernisation. The progress of modernisation is closely related to the pace of educational development. The spread of education, the preparation of educated and skilled citizens and training of intelligents' promote modernisation. The Indian society is the succession of a hoary heritage and inherits a rich culture. But unless it becomes alerty education, industrious, it cannot be modernised. In order to meet the challenges of national and international needs and conditions, education has to be geared and engineered accordingly.

Education for modernisation

Our education was originally meant for white-collar jobs and perceptible and impressive. Above fifty per cent of people belong to Scheduled Castes and Scheduled Tribes and about seventy per cent of people are below the poverty line. Unless education is made relevant to the life, needs and aspirations, it cannot be effective and successful. A large percentage of the present students in schools and colleges are first generation learners. In order to make education attractive and meaningful to them, new methods, materials and media are to be utilised. The composition of the intelligentsia must also change and now it should consist of competent persons, both men and women drawn from all strata of the society. The educated people must also represent from all vocations and disciplines like technical, scientific, skilled, artistic and so on. Modernised society must develop with the contributions from all concerned, particularly must also be of high standard. So, for maintaining adequate standard of education, research and science, a good number of major universities and centres of advanced learning should be developed in our country.

Modernisation does not mean complete isolation or segregation from the past traditions. It must be built on the past reflecting the needs of the present and vision of the future social order. India's prosperity and modernisation must be based on the moral and spiritual values enshrined in its culture. "Modernisation, if it is to be a living force, must derive its strength from the spirit. Modernisation aims, amongst other things at creating an economy of plenty which will offer, to every individual, a large of life and a wider variety of choices". Freedom of choices is very advantageous, but it depends on one's value system and motivation. The social, moral and spiritual values will greatly influence one's decisions for common good for selfish ends. Expansion of knowledge must be strengthened with these values.

It is felt that weakening of moral and spiritual values in the modern youths is creating many serious social problems and ethical as well as psychological conflicts. Therefore social workers and thinkers have suggested that knowledge and skills contributed by science and technology should be supplemented by values and insights associated with ethics and religion at its best. Inter-human and so on, should influence many of our decisions and choices. In short, value-judgment should orient our educational system. Right values are to be inculcated in the students at all stages of education. There has been growing sense of awareness about this responsibility after Independence.

For inculcation of values through education, we should draw freely from the confidently upon our own heritage as well as the traditions of other countries and the world culture as a whole. There are many values and elements in our national culture which will provide inspiration and solace to the modern society with all sorrows and sufferings, troubles and turmoils. Our national leaders like Mahatma Gandhi, Jawaharlal Nehru, Sri Aurobindo were inspired with passionate zeal and striving for social justice and national reconstruction largely from these sources. Thus it is necessary to re-evaluate and reinterpret our culture of the past from that point of view.

Lastly, it is desirable to conclude the issue of modernisation in India with particular reference to the following:

1. Eradication of mass illiteracy and ignorance.
2. Need for socio-political awakening.
3. Abolition of casteism, regionalism, linguism and communalism.
4. Emphasis on science and technology.
5. Equalisation of educational opportunities.
6. Introduction of compulsory primary education.

7. Development of right attitudes and values.

8. Expansion of social education.

With these in view, the entire educational machinery has to be geared to the solution of various problems . Now it has to operate on two fronts (i) children and (ii) adults. Although the constitutional Directive for providing compulsory primary education to all children in the age-group 6-14 years had not yet been realised, all attempts are being made to achieve this end during the 6th Five-Year Plan. Since India is known as the land of youths, it has rightly been observed that her "destiny is being shaped in her classrooms". That is why, universalisation of education within the shortest possible time is of utmost importance for effective modernisation.

Another front, adult or nonformal education is of crucial importance. Adults are directly involved in the national reconstruction and developmental works. The urgent need of educating the adults without waiting for school children to complete their education and participate in the developmental activities of the country has been laid stress by various international as well as national education authorities and experts. The social education or nonformal education programmes so much emphasised by the National Adult Education Programmes with effect from October 2, 1978 is of far-reaching consequences. But the strategies and techniques followed in implementing this programme need drastic change and the methods, media and materials adopted for such education should be renovated and developed for more effectiveness. Thus in order to make modernisation a real success and a dynamic process of social change, the role of education at all stages cannot be over-estimated.

3

Educational Reforms

Vernon Mallinson's major contribution to the standard literature of Education was first published in 1957. After several new editions it is still a popular text, widely used in the colleges and universities of many countries. And yet one must also record that Mallinson always encouraged an indulgence in one's formative discipline, seeing studies in education as a collaborative rather than a polymathic exercise. It is not only Mallinson and Bereday who have treated the "geographical factor" in a limited, deterministic and usually physical way. Indeed, all other major contributors to the standard literature of this field either adopt a very similar approach, or even fail to mention it at all. Again, there are mitigating circumstances. The image of the geographical factor is outdated is at least as much the fault of geographers as it is of comparativists. Despite the widespread and developing utilisation of land for educational purposes, very few geographers have been stimulated to apply modern techniques of spatial and locational analysis to these phenomena. It is not surprising therefore, that geography is viewed by many educationalists almost exclusively in physical terms, and even then altitudinal and scenic images predominate. Consequently, the geographical factor is seen as a constant, whereas in reality it is continually changing in temporal as well as in spatial terms.

Such an image represents a very positive and ingrained type of misconception. Nothing short of an immersion in modern geographical practices is likely to have very much effect on the perceptions of those accustomed to seeing geography as the backcloth rather than the stage. While it is easy to see how the image of geography has fossilised, given the politics and evolution of the school curriculum, the relative neglect of educational themes by professional geographers is nothing short of extraordinary. The main reason for the relative lack of interest in the past, and, despite the important reassessments in the scope and methodology of geography in recent years, the present, is probably the assumption by geographers and others that educational opportunity and provision are evenly distributed throughout the population.

To an educationist, acutely aware of the incidence of disparities of provision and performance, but unless and until the spatial skills of modern analytical geography are taken on board, the quality of that awareness is likely to be less than objective.

Modern education takes a dynamic view of spatial phenomena, however transitory, and shares with related social sciences such characteristics as: the establishment of a quantified data base; the employment of nomothetic models; the "issue-based approach" as a mode of entry; an awareness of the significance of the behavioural dimension. It is distinctive in applying such techniques spatially, and so long as education as a human activity remains a user of space it will have a geographical dimension to be analysed, and possibly thereby exploited to greater advantage in terms of economy and performance. Merely by relating the four techniques mentioned above to educational themes, the potential of a new geographical factor in comparative education becomes apparent.

From this basic application of everyday techniques of modern geography to educational themes, one may attempt to apply the structural components of geography, as perceived by contemporary exponents, to such themes. For this purpose, models by Haggett and Walford have been selected, and together with suggested applications.

It is clear that applications of the style and nature of modern geography that almost any fact could be applied to some aspect of education. So one would certainly agree with Rawstron that:

> There is an enormous field of research awaiting enquiry throughout the world.

Two simple examples will suffice at this stage to illustrate geographical dimensions and implications of educational provision, one urban and one basically, though not entirely, rural.

First, *sector analysis* in urban geography. The massive growth of towns and cities in developed and developing nations alike is a major geographical feature. Given the diffuse relationship between formal education and urbanity, it is not difficult to predict that not only would one find a concentration of educational provision in towns and cities, but also that in terms of status and quality there will be a gradient from urban to rural. Models have been devised to assist studies in urban growth, structure, decay and other characteristics of towns and cities. The general idea behind sector analysis is that certain, sometimes related, activities tend to cluster in distinctive areas of towns, and that there is a dynamic element in the growth and maintenance of such sectors which has to do with differential mobility and structural inertia. Most of this analysis has concentrated on clustering of industrial, commercial and residential features. Why not apply this concept, however crudely in the first instance, to education? Applied to the City of Leeds, for example, we find a clear concentration of "high status" educational land use extending north-west from the centre, indeed confined almost entirely to the narrow sector diverging between the A660 and the A65. Within this zone are located the vast majority of further and higher education institutions, including two of the largest universities and polytechnics in Britain, the most prestigious secondary schools, the teachers' centre and even the offices of the education authority.

A simple application of *distance decay function* to primary school enrolment in rural East Africa is also illustrated. As applied in this case, the analysis is concerned to find the "break-point" distance between home and school, beyond which a child would be deterred from enrolling or attending. The distance discovered as being crucial will almost certainly not be the same in respect of different routes, and reasons for this may or may not have to do with the incidence of additional spatial phenomena.

The direct effect of distance may be increased where sending a child to school is considered with the alternative of having the child at home to work on the farm or help with domestic chores, fetching water in particular. The further the child is from school, the more likely it is that keeping the child away from school is considered the more reasonable alternative.

This apparently simplistic observation is in reality a matter of major concern for providers and receivers of education in "third World" rural areas, for its resolution depends on more detailed research into further dimensions of spatial constraint, including the behavioural. The plotting of the results of such a function is at least a first step towards a more accurate understanding of the actual use of what may have been intended as a universal provision of educational opportunity.

As one of a number of geographical factors, does education have a particularly distinctive role? Spencer and Thomas see education systems as being "space adjusting techniques", because:

> they seek to create cultural uniformity and continuity over all the territory occupied by the society operating the educational system.

and Abler, Adams and Gould recognise this factor as crucial to the spatial integrity of any country when they say:

> Part of the information sector of a nation's space economy is neither product oriented or service orientated. Instead its job is to produce new knowledge, new application of ideas, or to transmit formalised bodies of knowledge and to train people in the knowledge business. Thus a nation's educational system together with its research and development effort forms a cornerstone for the entire society.

Such perceptions relate to the fields of cultural and political geography, but it is evident also that education, in the widest sense, is a massive economic exercise, a growth point in the modernisation of nations at all levels of development. Much of this expansion in advanced societies is not necessarily taking the traditional form of the establishment of centres of learning at fixed locations. With the provision of new media - the cybernetic revolution - and the massive availability of information for self-selection, the spatial implications of educational activity become more diffuse. Alongside the nonplace realm concept of the geographer runs what price describes as "multi-disciplined self-paced learning", creating new educational complexes and rendering an increasing proportion of plant obsolete. So the economic ramifications of different forms of educational contraction and expansion have significant effects well beyond the circle of those directly involved. For example, the multiplier effect of the establishment and operation of an institution of higher education can be considerable, with geographical consequences outside areas of specifically educational land use. This community and occupational enmeshment of educational space with other forms of space makes a clear case for the development of a "geographical of education" replacing the determinism of the geographical factor and capitalising on the generic relationship with comparative education in particular.

Before considering this relationship, especially with respect to the question of scale, a survey of selected literature will serve to illustrate the fact that there does exist a small but significant body of work that can be assigned to various components of this emergent sub-discipline illustrated. For the most part, the pieces of work in question have arisen independently and not as part of any awareness of the building of a sub-discipline as such on the part of the respective authors. It is hoped that the following sequence of surveys will serve to enhance the perception of their kinship and of the distinctive contribution of a geographical approach.

Literature survey

With many developing countries, regional education data in Costa Rica is difficult to obtain or inadequate in nature for studies leading to possibilities of rural and community development. Techniques are therefore considered by cox for using the school, and the school-based community, as the spatial context for the receipt and application of socio-economic information. In reality, this means the catchment area, both in theoretical and effective terms, for each school. In this way, some of the generalisations of data based on political areas not coincident with local community watersheds are avoided. Cox concludes that this technique can be rapid, inexpensive and reliable in obtaining: "a closer approximation to the regional reality". It also has that necessary contact with local attitudes and practices so vital to the grafting of any developmental scheme that may follow.

In this chapter consideration is given to the general applicability of geographical approaches to the study of educational phenomena, and within this there is a concentration on: regional differences in educational opportunity; the location of schools; the spacing of schools. Stress is laid on the problems of researching such apparently quantifiable themes, by examining also the degree of colonial penetration; parental aspiration; religious differences and other social disparities. These qualifying factors are related to the quantified patterns of educational provision to form an integrated picture of local and regional infrastructure. The crucial significance of roads, and the application of the idea of distance decay function are also features of this widely ranging article. In the final resort, Gould acknowledges that: "the final decision is a political one", and concludes that a wider perspective would be given to planning teams by the inclusion of a geographer.

Hones sees the role of the geographer in the spatial planning of educational systems as being concerned with "the location of individual establishments, their pattern of distribution, and the interacting relationships which comprise the network-as well as relating this to the surface, physical and human, on which the system operates". Hones in effect finds that the application of geographical techniques to educational patterns and practices revels so great a level of environmental influence that "the use of a theoretical model can be questioned". Local attitudes are also seen to be variable, and crucial to the understanding of the pattern. So this is not really a repudiation of the geographical factor, but a call for greater sophistication and qualification in the spatial analysis of education, and for more detailed case studies to range alongside the theory.

Maxfield illustrates the capacity of techniques of spatial study and linear programming to enable administrators to reach better decisions concerning the micro and macro planning of school districts. Application is made to the specific problems of overcrowding, desegregation and the assessment of future needs. A dynamic spatial approach is obvious in such statements as: "Within the framework of a multi-locational supply and multi-locational demand problem, the transportation routine solves problems where the end result is to minimise a function of distance when many alternative choices of routing are available". A case study of the application of such techniques to a school district in Georgia illustrates clearly the need for a local dimension in the co-ordination of short and long term needs and objectives in the spatial planning of educational provision.

Location as a factor in educational opportunity

In this study, explanation is sought through geographical means, for the immense variations in different aspects of education between the various Local Education Authorities of England and Wales. Rawstron indicates that these cannot be explained merely as inevitable concomitants of a form of decentralisation. If they represent complicated local differences in patterns of facility and attitude, then geographical techniques should help in bringing these to light. He shows how spatial approaches can be made to selected sectors of provisions, e.g. "opting out of the maintained sector", and "staying on into further education". Problems of data are raised in a somewhat similar fashion to Geipel, but he comments: "It should be emphasised in conclusion that the scope for research extends from the micro-study of data for individual school catchment areas to macro analysis leading to the discernment of broad spatial trends". This is a challenge to comparativists to be willing to operate at various levels of scale.

The geography of education and educational planning

This is a most valuable study, and one that will become to be seen as an important formative agent in the establishment of the sub-discipline "geography of education" Ryba refers to the dearth of research in this field as being: "paradoxical in view of the very high proportion of geographers in most countries who devote themselves on graduation either to education or to planning". This may be symptomatic of our obsession with specialisation, leaving a general inability to grasp interdisciplinary links and carry forward expertise gained at one stage of one's educational career to another. Ryba considers three approaches to be especially worthy of further consideration: the geographical examination of factors underlying education; the examination of the spatial patterns of educational phenomena; the role of education as a factor influencing the geographical patterns of other social and cultural phenomena. He goes further than Gould in relating spatial aspects of education to other space users, and in predicting in a similar way to price that educational activity has a profound and probably increasing influence on patterns of settlement and networks of activity.

Regional research on education

Bundes lander of West Germany highlights a very real problem for any researcher into the potentially embarrassing issue of educational disparities, namely dependence on the co-operation of the authorities presiding over such irregularities. In this case the authorities, once alerted to the object of the exercise, in effect took over the studies and cut out the original workers. Consequently, Geipel advocates individual research at a very detailed local level on a case-study basis, in the hope that: "new aspects of geographic theory will be developed ensuring the continued importance of the Geography of Education.

Spatial variations in educational provision in colombia

This is a comment on significant educational disparities

between urban and rural area; within and between urban areas; between different administrative areas. The influence of a strong private sector on public provision is noted in spatial terms, and the fundamental significance of regional disparities arising from the decentralisation of funding is regarded as crucial, together with differential local capacities of teacher education. Gilbert indicates the particular ability of educational development to stimulate rural based growth, social mobility and economic development.

Schools in transition

In particular, an assessment is made of "residential segregation" as being "a most fundamental facet of the spatial structure of the society", and consideration is given to various informal as well as official movements acting in opposition to the location and racial composition of schools in the state of Mississippi. This chapter is a valuable insight for outsiders of the dynamics of educational manipulation in social and spatial terms as operable within the socio-political framework of the U.S.A. Lowry concludes: "Integrated education might be fundamental to an integrated society, but in the contemporary United States residential desegregation probably is more so". This is so, especially in view of local funding of educational provision in the U.S.A.

Secondary school admissions policies in eastern Africa

Secondary schools admissions policies are contrasted between Kenya, Uganda, Zambia and Tanzania. The author outlines regional issues in each of these areas that affect the disparate patterns of enrolment. Differential access in terms of tribal concentrations and variations in colonisation and missionary activity in the past are considered. In effect the establishment of a network of secondary opportunity as a crucial factor in overcoming local and regional bias in social opportunity, and in the building of unified nations, is the burden of the study. It is of interest too in comparing the international differences, especially in view of the common experience of British Colonial administration. The role of an anthropological perspective also comes through. It is concluded that the integrating role will be better achieved through day, rather than boarding secondary schools, though this could also create further rural disadvantage.

The object here is to emulate the care and calculation over location so evident in the economic sphere. The central issue is the minimising of journeys to school in time and distance, so as to reduce the influence of distance decay. The problem arises from disparities in provision, and these are illustrated in relation to population clusters in the parish, by the application of a spatial equilibrium model under linear programme. The selection of additional locations is achieved through the application of the Weberian triangle to each area of deficit. The combination of these techniques deals with the problem of the duality of spatial form and social process. The value of the study to educational planning lies in the quantitatively measured cost of alternative policies, and also in the social implications of spatial considerations - an efficient yet humane input resource allocation; in this case, of accessible primary schools in a developing country.

Having commented on the curious neglect of territorial nations in comparative education, this chapter sets out to illustrate territorial inequalities in education at different scales, from intercontinental to local. The enormity of disparities in literacy levels as between the various continents precedes a more detailed discussion on less extreme, but nonetheless startling, disparities at international levels within Europe, and arising from a more secure statistical base. For international disparities Ryba takes the case of England and Wales, and with special reference to enrolment in the post-compulsory sector he comments on the general correlation between educational deprivation and other forms of social disadvantage. This is further developing countries, introducing the notion of an educational gradient. For the local dimension he selects intra-urban disparities, showing that this issue goes far beyond the classically simplistic "slums and suburbs" dichotomy. In questioning the neglect of the character of education in many comparative studies. Ryba succeeds in illustrating the practical potential of a more sophisticated territorial approach.

Education of nineteenth century towns and cities

An attempt is made here to focus on the incidence of disparities in educational provision within urban areas by examining selected cases, especially London and Bootle, during the last century. By concentrating on a period of both rapid urban and suburban development and also of the emergence of a universal provision of elementary education, Marsden succeeds in illustrating the interconnections between education and other strands of the urban fabric and society. In particular, he examines education in terms of the evolution of "secluded social areas" within towns, that is to say, residential zones correlated with social class. Even within such zones he is able to show very localised nuances in respect of both private and state schooling. Catchments, journeys to school, sexism, fee disparities and hierarchies are utilised in order to illustrate spatial patterns. In conclusion he clearly demonstrates the dominance of general patterns of social disparity and deprivation over the potentially ameliorative or even compensatory qualities of educational provision.

The main object here is to consider the effects of national manpower and education policies on remote rural communities, with particular reference to the role of migration. The research is based on both documentary and empirical methods, and looks at five communities especially in terms of attitudes to education. The relationship between educational planning and provision is examined, clearly illustrating rural disadvantage as well as the contrast between the attitudes and perceptions of urban planners and those of peasant communities. The section on education and migration examines rural returnees as well as emigres, and shows a generally higher educational level among both groups of migrants as opposed to the "sedentary" rural populations. It is made clear that migration does not seem to have damaged the rural community, rather the reverse, and that the main force to be confronted is the inertia of spatial disparity in educational provision- the resistance of the rural/urban dichotomy.

The emergence of an educational system

From a brief initial comment on the capacity of a geography of education to include traditional geographical factors; spatial variations; education as a geographical factor, the author applies such perspectives to an analysis of the character of educational development in colonial Massachusetts. He looks in turn at the origin, support and control of educational institutions in that colony in comparison with the position obtaining in England at the time of colonization. He explains significant departures from the then metropolitan pattern, through the themes of distance and movement, migration and diffusion, and core-periphery forces-all, of course, spatial concepts. He also introduces the behavioural dimension in respect of the reaction of settlers and pioneer communities to their perception of the American wilderness. McPartland concludes that the adoption of a geographical/ecological perspective on the formative influences of American education that persist so strongly, albeit differentially, at the present day, helps to challenge the conventional view of ideological dominance in the formulation of an education system.

Application

If located on the application of the Haggett or Walford models, there would be a clustering in the areas relating to applied geography-planning. While this demonstrates the practical and dynamic possibilities of the emergent geography of education, it also indicates the scope for many other applications. One, for example, is represented in the above selection, namely the historical geography of education, and the last-named has in fact made a number of other significant contributions to this dimension. Other facets likely to reward further geographical analysis would clearly be migration and education; diffusion of knowledge; school mapping; intra-urban disparities and patterns.

In many detailed ways, the researches and techniques of modern geography can, and are beginning to, add their particular contribution to the armoury of educational studies in general, but why the particular relevance and potential for comparative education? For this we must return to the aforementioned generic relationship between comparative education and geography, so well endorsed by spolton and Fletcher, though one must have reservations about Fletcher's apparent contention that geography subsumes comparative education. For a more realistic view of their kinship one may turn to one of Vernon Mallinson's contemporaries and fellow developer of education in the colleges and universities, George Bereday. That Bereday's perception of geography extends beyond the physical dimension is shown by the fact that among the three candidates shortlisted by him as suitable foster-parents for the fledgling "education" is political geography. Certainly it is at the geopolitical scale of the nation state that the balance of comparative educational study has been undertaken. This is not surprising, since the formative phase of the discipline was a response to the development of official educational units of the emergent, competitive and imitative national units of the nineteenth century. Indeed, a modest geographical scale and a unitary education system are implied in the amalgam of the five factors reckoned by Hans to be necessary attributes of the ideal nation.

While in their detailed application the various facets of modern geography can serve comparative studies in education, it is in that most fundamental element of geographical perception, the question of scale, that it can most profitably inform. A glance at the fifteen studies summarised above is sufficient to show that their scale of reference ranges from the individual school and catchment, through local, national, regional and international levels, according to their particular concerns. It is true that some leading comparativists are keen to consult the entrails as well as the carcase. As Holmes has observed: "The main thrust of comparative education research can be accommodated within an ecological approach".

Undoubtedly a more sophisticated and updated applications of the "geographical factor" will assist. Both ecological and political parameters can range fro the individual to the global, in respect of educational system. On the *political* side, it is easier to operate an analysis at various scales because of the discretion of political hierarchies which in many nations carry attendant and distinctive functions in respect of educational administration and provision. Hence the data behind ;such revealing studies of educational disparities within England as those of Taylor and Ayres, and Coates, Johnston and knox. Also into this category of scale fall the excellent studies of regional disparities in educational development carried out by the International Institute for Educational Planning. There would seem to be considerable scope for comparative study here, the politico-spatial picture having been provided.

Thus far, the term "regional" has been used to refer to divisions within nations-perhaps "provincial" would be better, for regional can also mean a part of the world comprising a number of nations. In some cases, clusters of nations have degree of interdependence in respect of education. This is especially the case with groups of small countries such as exist in the tropical island zones. In addition to obvious problems of political geography and status, there are other spatial issues to be confronted in terms of the logistics of co-operation, and of both I have written elsewhere. Federations provide good opportunities for comparison between components in respect of education; and as Grant has pointed out in respect of Britain, much ground could be made up here. Indeed, it may well be that, given the relative ease of the data issue within a federal state, some of the methodological issues of comparative study could be worked through. At any rate, there is considerable scope for sub-national and intra-federal research, supported by standard techniques of spatial and locational analysis.

While the ecological approach must be mindful of the political strand, it also offers the possibility of a grater range of variables becoming available for comparative work, and a change to investigate the dynamics of educational systems at various scales, again from individual to international. This would of course need collaboration with anthropological techniques, since a persistence is evident in patterns of educational disparity operating both within and across political and administrative boundaries, that would seem to qualify as a cultural feature. As put by Ryba there is often:

> a complex territorially differentiated factor in educational achievement which may be best summed up as the cultural traditions in the territorial context.

Though such patterns are, at most, provincial in scale, they would seem to go some way towards the concept of national character in education, much favoured and promoted by Vernon Mallinson.

At a similar dimension of scale, and certainly more susceptible of comparative analysis, would be attempts to unravel the dynamic involvement of the educational component of what geographers term a "regional complex". That is to say a geographical area with a dynamic identity, as opposed to a politically delimited zone. A regional complex is normally the sphere of influence of a very large urban area, normally a city, and it is unlikely that the continually changing area involved will correspond with any one zone of educational administration. High status in the urban hierarchy is gained by the incidence of very special services, examples of which in the educational field would be a polytechnic or a university, and these would normally be a component of a regional complex. As has been mentioned above, such institutions have important multiplier effects in economic terms, and their case against Government directed cuts in 1981/2 in Britain has normally included an illustration of the local and regional effects of such reductions on non-academic employment. Comparison of a British case with that of the establishment of the Louvain Catholic University, for example, would certainly be informative in terms of regional complex analysis.

Universities, given their status internationally, provide in their networks of operation, a degree of convergence between the political and ecological dimensions of spatial comparative analysis. Such convergence is crucial in the operation of regional universities, such as the University of the West Indies and the University of the South Pacific, which are shared, albeit unequally, by a number of nations. So, in addition to having important community functions at a local scale, universities:

> are disseminators and producers of knowledge in their own nations, playing increasingly important roles in technological societies. They are part of an international knowledge system as well, interacting with institutions abroad.

In the same way as spatial systems analysis could be employed in comparative studies of university operations at various scales of reference, so it could be employed in respect of other sectors of educational activity. Whether it be politically or ecologically based, the capacity of the analytical tools of modern geography to accommodate the multi-scale context is at the disposal of any comparative educationist aware of the potential and conversant with the techniques.

The changing educational context

There is, of course, no need for academic interests and other enthusiasms to justify themselves with a useful purpose - at least, in all cases. The study of pond life, of etymology, of place-names, or indeed ethnology may arise from spontaneous interest and continue with that emphasis. More systematic information and insights, and perhaps utility for some practical application, may result directly or indirectly; but that outcome was not part of an original purpose.

Some criticism might be levelled against such pursuits if they absorbed time and resources which ought to be spent on other, more urgent, matters; or if those urgent matters were grievously neglected in research centres - as the physical sciences, the life sciences, and the modern human sciences were long neglected in universities while theological and similar abstractions occupied gifted minds. Such a "treason of the clerks" still taints some Latin countries universities and a few departments elsewhere; but as a rule dilettantism in the modern world is offset by human concern and a strong sense of professional obligation. What Americans have recognised as the "public service" function of higher education for over a century inheres in many learned investigations, and is certainly marked in what we all now accept as the teaching responsibility of higher education. In that respect comparative studies of education have a particular commitment.

Today's context - especially since the multiple crises of the early 1970 - surrounds and pervades the perceptions of every teacher, student, and researcher. For the comparative educator this altered context not merely means that there is a wider span of countries, systems and populations engaged in formal education and indeed its evolution or reform to be studied but it has also introduced a quite different horizon of concerns and a reordering of priorities within any study. Our own experience alone would insist on that; but we are not alone in the relevance of our experience. The experience and insights of far more people on far more occasions over a whole life-span are now recognised as the proper test-bed of theories and experiments once expounded with priestly assurance. Indeed, not only "feedback" to "experts" but effective "participation" by a much wider representation of humanity are now seen as essential for successful scholarship.

The later 1970s and the opening 1980s have established a new climate as well as a new context for scholarship of every kind. Comparative studies of education naturally share and are affected by the circumstances which constrain and condition us all materially - not just in resources or in the data before us but more in our appreciation of what can, and must be done because comparative studies are studies of education, concerned with ameliorative activity.

Whereas the study of philosophy of even of animal species and communities still keeps us "outside" the object of our research even when our study requires some empathy with the behaviour we investigate, an effective study of education does not allow us the luxury of distant detachment. Of course we try to obtain objective data, to categorise them "scientifically" and to process or compute them in a way that makes them universally relevant or at least intelligible; but there are two special pitfalls for the student of education which do not beset students in other areas of inquiry. The first is that involvement of the observer in the process of observation has been preconditioned by his own idiomatic upbringing and educational expectations - quite apart from his academic preoccupations. The second is that everyone's expectations of educations have undergone a marked change over the past two or three decades. That change has a special bearing on questions of reform, urgently demanded on so many fronts.

Pressures for reform

Let us look first at what we might call the outer, environmental conditioning of reform. The context of public opinion the institutional nexus, and occupational prospects must all be right before any reform can "take on", still more, - "take off". We have all seen this truism repeatedly in failed French educational reform. Mitterand revives and refurbishes Haby; before him there were reforms stampeded through by de Gaulle after May 1968; and before that there were Langevin and Wallon in 1947 and the Compagnons de 1 Universite Nouvelle in 1918 - all with substantially the same master-plan and many similar details, but all waiting for a war, a civil crisis or an electoral turnabout to give, first the impetus for acceptance and, secondly, the socio-economic and technological matrix for a new educational life-style.

No less important than the domestic ecology for education in one country is a wider type of conditioning influence. The years soon after 1945 were marked by opening doors and by wider recruitment. From the 1950s to the early 1960s the mood was one of confident expansion - expansion of provision, of staffing, of curricula. Alongside the necessary structural reorganisation and facilitation of access and transfer there developed a glorification of method - sometimes spuriously attaching to itself the suffix "-ology"

What was the point of this preoccupation? It was symptomatic not only of academic inflation, which over the years has deflated esteem for even genuine studies of education, but also of a concern for "process", which in North America produced "input-process-output" models and "cost-effectiveness" scrutiny and other supposed mechanisms for "efficiency". Why put the word "efficiency" in quotation marks? Because concern was not with effectiveness of education as perceived and profited by at the receiving end. The mechanics of the systems proposed depended on the concept of people doing things to other people, especially doing civilising things to less civlised people so that they could be assimilated, or encouraged to conform, or be "predicted" as manpower, and so forth.

True, most of us really need better management in our professional services; but until the end of the 1960s or even into the early 1970s it was not realised that management in education was special to education, or that management was not enough. It is no use "transmitting" culture or "delivering the goods" if they are left on the doorstep. At least as early as the Berkeley remonstrances of 1964, the "flower power" phenomenon and other symptoms of rejection made it clear in highly schooled countries like Sweden and Denmark, with their respective problems of truancy and free school(s), that educational endeavour fails unless the learner accepts and identifies himself with what is offered - and, indeed, takes it further in his own idiom. During the past decade that same message has come back to us repeatedly from Third World countries. We are just beginning, too, to recognise its full relevance to the case of our own "lower orders", to most young adults, and to the unemployed.

So the early post-1945 comparative studies of structural reforms with their "juxtapositions" and tabulations and confident predictions that this or that "model" would prevail in retrospect look like preliminary classifications before an effective study could take place of what really went on both within and without school systems. "Competency" training of teachers and "efficient" training of heads and administrators were both, no doubt, pre-requisities to something; but to what? Obviously, to the effective self-education of the student, particularly in the later secondary stages and in life afterwards. During international researches and many discussions in the early 1970s it was difficult to secure appreciation of what "effective" education meant - at least among teachers and administrators. In several languages there is no separate word for "effective", to distinguish it from the notion of "efficiency"; and in international statistics the word "effective" was used simply to denote a body enrolled in a classroom - nothing to do with a mind engaged and a real-life commitment afterwards. But students themselves knew only too well what "effective" education meant for them; and the majority of the age-group not enrolled, or "failing" within or dropping out of the system, knew even more acutely what was "effective" in formal education and what was not. They also knew only too well how much education was left out of formal schooling.

Hence it was deeply important to investigate not what was supposed to go on, or what providers intended to lay before the populace, but what actually was perceived as going on at the receiving end. Several international investigations of "the view from inside" began in the early 1960s, including the 3-year, 5-nation, study of Post-Compulsory Education undertaken by the Comparative Research Unit at King's College in the University of London. In most instances it was the very first time that teachers - let alone students - had ever been asked for their opinion and insights. Though the LEA investigation of Achievement in Mathematics, directed and edited by Torsten Husen, in many ways blazed a trail for empirical research in comparative studies, it was marred in so far as it emphasised the aspects of manipulation and control by providers. So were many of the ideas then current in OECD and the International Institute for Educational Planning. Elsewhere, "computable models" of school systems were proposed. The big turnabout followed consumer reaction, which was sometimes disastrous for education in the short term as parents and electors took issue with providers, although in the long run comparative studies of students' reactions may help us to a far truer understanding of education's need and feasibilities today.

Let us look at the same shift of emphasis in relation to the notion of "partnership". In Sweden, France, and many other countries with centralised administrations, there was no nonsense about "partnership" in determining educational policy and content. In Britain the tradition to "partnership" was exemplified in the sharing of provision, expense, and day-to-day responsibility for ultimate satisfactoriness. But until 1977 and the Taylor Report there was little official recognition that the "partnership" included parents, though of course some local authorities did so. The notion that school students might also share in school government had an even tougher passage, despite the fact that at 18 they can help to elect the country's government, or, if employed, participate in works' councils' affairs from the age of 16. The "partnership" envisaged was therefore one of managing the provision, as though from on high, or externally.

The related word "participation" is also worth examination. In many publications from OECD, the Council of Europe, and other international agencies, the word was used as a synonym for "enrolment". The only sharing considered was that of taking up whatever was set out by others, at least in education. That seems odd, especially when participation in a game or similar activity implies interlocking and relevant activities, perhaps even teamwork.

That notion of really countries for something within the entire system was certainly taken up by countless American school boards during the 1970s. The United States system of administration has long devolved responsibility for most educational decisions, including costs, on to such local boards, where parents may be the boards' direct electors. But the "grass rots" rebellion against superintendents, management and teachers' practices during the 1970s introduced demands for "accountability", cuts in school taxes, and some growing preference for private high schools - especially as a result of nationwide comparisons with other districts or other states of the Union. International comparisons by Husen et. al. in the LEA surveys had prepared the ground but had not directly occasioned such parental distress or legislative onslaught on the entire state system. All of these and related phenomena exemplify a public demand for real participation in the process of education which is beginning to be world-wide.

The ecological framework

At the present stage of international comparative study, it is vital to recognise the experiential dimension in our investigations and teaching. By that I mean the element of profiting from experience - our own and others' - not only in order to understand better, but also in order to teach theorists and paper reformers what actually goes on when educational reforms are embarked upon. It is not simply that the world as a whole has moved on in its general experience, though that is tellingly true, but it is even more important to recognise that education in particular has moved on and to acknowledge two things: (a) that education essentially is a matter of organising experience into a personal system; (b) that this occurs within an idiomatic but evolving "educational system" - part of a wider cultural pattern, and within a larger social/economic/technological system which "makes sense" according to the perceptions of that place, population, or occasion. It is our business as comparative students of education to know the realities of characteristic systems and subsystems of education, to feel within the occasions and crises of judgement as experienced by the protagonists, and of course to adduce from one situation to another what may be helpful parallels or interpretations. In short, we must "teach" in the sense of offering aids to judgement, to more effective participation, and to reform.

Thus our function is distinct from, though complementary to, that of students of politics whose concern is to show and classify examples of the interplay of power, or of sociologists demonstrating that in all societies there are particular groups and pressures. True, pressure groups may use or frustrate education in order to exercise power or to re-order society; but the human beings involved in the process can accept or reject these manipulations in ways which we should know from an educational angle. Educational systems formally set up, or the more diffuse folk-ways and local or topical "inside view", positively teach their populations to react in particular ways. These are part of our stock-in-trade, as foreign languages and comparative linguistic studies are the stock-in-trade of the comparative philologist. We know them with some precision; we teach about them; we know characteristic situations and present trends. Some generalisations are permissible - as hypotheses only, to be substantiated or refuted with reference to precise situations. Not for us the "ideal types" of the sociologist. People do not react that way, even in the mass - and least of all in the inevitably intimate encounter which education constitutes by its very nature.

It has been said with some truth that any given curriculum is 100 different curricula for 100 different people. So much for what we might call "lateral" comparisons within a tiny bit of a system. Still more, continually over time and in a series of evolving contexts, we all re-engage ourselves and whatever we have learned. To some extent that evolution is personal; in other respects it depends on our group contacts, each one of which obviously form part of a great complex of connections and communications. The point of repeating this truism is that many standard studies of education pay far too little attention to the dimensions: (a) the general ecological dynamics surrounding "the process" at any time or place; and (b) the long-term completion or frustration of the formal educational process. Perhaps more telling in the long run is the study of what that formal process omits, or fails to take account of in the formative context surrounding it. The feeding into our study of fresh perceptions, unanswered questions, perhaps even questions un-asked hitherto, presents a potent challenge to comparative specialists. In this matter as well as in more traditional ways we can make reform attempts more realistic.

Nor should it be supposed simplistically that the reactions and questions just referred to occur with spontaneous clarity to individuals and groups, or that because of our common humanity there are universal responses and needs in education at any one time. As I have pointed out elsewhere, thoughts and preferences in education clothe our minds idiomatically like language. Language is learned - and taught - unconsciously and consciously by parents, peer groups, and day-to-day communications, long before formal instruction in a language takes place. In that sense, educational expectation and preference are taught too. It is very hard to un-think ourselves from our schooling, and still more to dissociate educational essentials from the apparatus, traditions, and intentions of the schooling industry. We think and talk its language because we have been taught it. Are there alternatives? Could there be alternatives because of changed technological/occupational necessity, or because of altered occupational/career expectations? these are potent questions for comparative study. especially now.

National character

Before coming to a closer analysis of these things, we may give a bow to Vernon Mallinson and "national character". A few critics on some occasions have taken a swipe at the notion of "national character". I have yet to find Vernon Mallinson saying that "national character" is, so to speak, acquired through the genes. We all know that, to go no further, Western Europeans living in rather flat lands open to the sea and on migration routes have been invaded time and again by sundry bands of youngish men who hardly even brought many women with them. They found them on the spot. Where there have been larger migrations of both sexes, they have eventually merged with or been swamped in turn by others - often the indigenous population, itself mongrel. Genetically, in most countries, we are all mongrels in varying degree. Yet through language differentiation, cultural and trading contacts, religions, motherhood, and other teaching institutions, we have in sundry ways learned to recognise and prize ourselves as members of tribes, nations, or whatever. We teach our children all about it, build fences, and resist or even attack neighbours. Since nation-states developed, and especially since formal school systems, often backed up by religious or socio-economic apparatus, were nationally invested with colossal powers of at least hidden persuasion, we have certainly been imbued with the notion of corporate character; and in our less conscious smugness or prejudices we bloat ourselves with the myth. Myth perhaps it is, in any totally objective sense, except that it really exists as a form of self-recognition - just like "class", in fact, which the sociologists accepts while rejecting the notion of "national character" as a system of self-ascription.

Myth it may be like Hitler and Rosenberg's myth of the master-race; but as a justification for particular kinds of indoctrination it is still an educational phenomenon to reckon with, if nothing else. Anyone who has been inside a situation where "national character" dominates consideration of educational aims and practices, as for example, in Afrikaner society, is left in no doubt of its potency in educational decisions, and in the fanatical adherence of many young embers. Not dissimilarly, we witness a rising appeal to nationhood and "national character" in many revolutionary nations. Iran's overweening national pride is not simply in the Islamic complement of its revolution; it does not forget the former glories of the Persian empire. Indeed, in England too, we still suffer from hidden or overt appeals to a supposed "national character" - not only in resisting dictatorial regimes far away but in being too "gentlemanly" to take educational account of the technological revolution in our midst.

Pressure for change and new educational frontiers

That technological metamorphosis of our time is of urgent concern to comparative students of education, and above all to those endeavouring to assist reform. The interface between national systems and internationally comparative considerations is more contentious than it has ever been. Moreover, the shifts in technological and educational emphasis between the era of heavy industrialisation and its associated commerce on the one hand and the microprocessor world of communications on the other are full of profound challenges for comparative study, both of educational responses as it actually happens and of projections for the future. Projections and planning in considerable detail are now part of the data before us.

Altered expectations of young adults - in school or college, in "the transition from school to work", in unemployment, and in returning to education and/or training - open up vistas of comparative investigation without previous example.

Furthermore, associated changes have brought about huge migrations of underprivileged workers into hitherto well-settled systems, with resulting problems of multicultural education - even for previously self-satisfied monocultures - and numerous internal problems of urban decay, flight to the suburbs, and so forth. Hardly any of these problems were recognised as even contingent fields of comparative study a generation ago, when the foundation studies of our discipline were established. Our comparative commitment must therefore be not simply lateral in some contemporary sense, but developmental and prospective too.

Since, as teachers no less than as scholars, we care so much for effective education, we must now pay far more attention to the receiving end - indeed, we must think of it not as a "receiving end" but as a situation where education begins. That is particularly so when we examine in the industrialised countries all those frontier situations where a new educational style is demanded. These manifestly include: the huge and varied increase in the enrolled over-16s in many countries, latterly accentuated by unemployment; the intermittent experience of paid employment and unemployment which now characterises the entire 16-25 population in the OECD countries of Western Europe generally, and in urban centres around the world in particular; the need to "catch up" with education and/or training at this level, though not at the usual age; and the case of new demand from hitherto neglected social categories such as migrants, girls, country people, and the old.

In the less industrialised countries and in the Third World generally, educational needs are now expressed in terms alien to those familiar in the formal education industry of the industrialised "West" and North. No longer is it sufficient to think in terms of "feedback" from these frontier regions of education. Our study must now be based upon the "view from inside", shared even for academic purposes with the local participants, and shared still more if we are to help in educational development and reform.

There are important ways in which all systems of schooling have become frontier areas in industrialised countries too. Reform must be radical and continuous, from our inner concepts outwards through our institutions and practices - not just for reasons of social amelioration and so forth, though these are integral to our continuing civilisation, but also for reasons of technological necessity. School systems as we know them are largely by-products of industrialisation, as H.C. Barnard and others have reminded us.

Following systematisation by Horace Mann and others in the United States, with mass availability of high schools and higher education in due course, the expansion of most forms of education throughout the industrialised world has been based on assumptions of assimilating people into the cultural and occupational mainstream of the host society, according to the ability and readiness of those being assimulated as well as in processing people as described earlier. The big reorientation is necessitated by what I have called the "third technological/educational phase". Others, like Daniel Bell, have spoken of a "post-industrial" or a "communications" society. Whatever the name, today's society and industries call for a much wider range of aptitudes and qualities, varied fields of interest and knowledge, differently developed and constantly re-adapted skills. In place of much compliant convergence, adaptive divergence and judgement are continually needed. Furthermore, this continuum of re-learning and re-creating is spread over a lifetime. This idiom or phase of education recognises the provisional or conditional status of the present state of knowledge or understanding.

Obviously, too, microprocessors and computer-assisted diffusion and analysis of knowledge, almost incalculably accelerated in little more than a decade, both demand and facilitate the participation and relevance of many people and activities not so far considered as partners in the educational process. The crumbling of industrial/occupational structures since the early 1970s, combined with the redistribution of much of the world's industry to new locations, had brought unemployment and job-changes into near-normal expectation in all the heavily industrialised countries of the Western World. At the same time, the "communications society" has thrust new concepts of learning relationships and feasibilities right down into the primary school stage - with, of course, a perspective of electronically supported learning and relearning throughout life. More than any change since formal education became a major state commitment, this challenge demands complete rethinking of educational aims and practice. For comparative studies of education this metamorphosis challenges our supply of data, our analysis of aims, and our skills in reassessing all learning relationships - not just once for all time, but in a commitment of unforeseeable duration and complexity. By the same token, it puts our studies at the very centre of any reform plans.

All effective education now must be a preparation for uncertainty, for responsible participation rather than indifferentism. Educational development and planning too must take the same stance, in preparation for varied and flexible response to ever-changing "crises" "Predictions", "laws" and expectations of convergent assimilation have no place in our study - if they ever had. We need careful study of what is, what is moving by way of response and experiment, what is planned for, and how the implementation proceeds in the world's national and cultural workshops. The microprocessor revolution and the advent of a "communications society" mean that the world shares technological apparatus and opportunities as never before; but by the same token a plurality of responses is as evident as the plurality of fashions on our streets, indeed more so because cultural individuality is not only prized but persistently taught and identified with. Who could expect one thousand million Chinese to be Russified, Americanised or even internationally neutered in culture - no matter what technologies are imported? Who could therefore expect education to have other than a national base, with national experimentation, and a latter day sense of being "central" no less than in the days of the "Central Kingdom".

Nonetheless, within each of the national systems still responsible by law and with financial responsibility for so much of the world's schooling and the educative media, pluralism is growing not only as a self-evident feature of daily life but as a desideratum in education. We do not seek a "melting-pot" or a farrago any more; we recognise that a multiplicity of perceptions and probably values too is essential to true civilisation. In search of whatever human essence may be we maintain the great conversation of mankind with comparative scholarship, as well as civilised acceptance of others' complementariness to our own perceptions and practices.

4

Variant Aims Administration in Education

It should now be clear that not only is the problem of education a new one for each succeeding generation, but also that the various social systems of the European nations as a whole were more than ripe for change as the last two world wars swept across them. Again the effective agents in this preparation for change have been: the growth of science; the growth of invention; the growth of industrial organization; the extension of education; and an imperative demand for equality of opportunity for all. There has also been a steady but determined move towards the idea of an education which will apply to the whole man: body, intellect, emotion, imagination. In this respect the twentieth century has heralded the conscious application to matters educational of our new knowledge of human behaviour, of child development, of cultural anthropology and of sociology. And in actual practice not only has the whole field of education been under review, but close attention has also been paid to personnel relationships in industry, to community organization, to government administrative practices, and to the content of mass media instruction. Our main purpose in this present chapter will be to show that, as different styles and manners of thinking are distributed amongst the nations, so are there different methods of approach adopted towards problems that are common to all the nations; problems concerning the vast extension of educational facilities that are being planned in all countries without exception; problems concerning the demand for equality of educational opportunity for all; problems concerning the relation of education to society.

For it is evident that education is part of a greater whole and cannot act in independence of it. All life is education, and—as Aldous Huxley pertinently reminds us—" life is a whole and desirable changes in one department will not produce the results anticipated from them unless they are accompanied by desirable changes in all other departments." Education is a part of life which is deliberately controlled, and in which experiences are developed according to a conscious plan. That is to say, the pattern of education is determined by the needs of society as a whole, and that society—no matter how willingly receptive it may be to the ideas of the educational philosophers—cannot wait for the results of philosophical speculation to crystallize themselves out into a conscious programme that can be faithfully applied to serve immediate needs and interests and to meet the challenge of the times. The State must have a dogmatic philosophy and must act upon it, a philosophy which confidently affirms something definite about the origin, the destiny, and the nature of man, and which provides a broad and sure basis for the elaboration of an educational system that will meet to the fullest all the demands the State is impelled to put upon it.

None the less, though because of all this we expect the aims of education to differ from country to country, we must acknowledge—as far as the U.S.A. and the democracies of Western Europe are concerned—that there is a certain common core factor of educational aims typified by what we might describe as Conservatism, Education for Citizenship and Education for Christian Salvation. By the conservative aim we mean an attempt at the conservation and perpetuation of the funded capital of past experience, the assurance of cultural continuity. Education for citizenship implies a firm belief in the democratic way of life and argues that the educational programme shall prepare all future citizens of a given State to play a full and active and responsible part in shaping and controlling the future of the State. Education for Christian salvation affirms a belief in a way of life which, whilst by no means basing itself on the tenants or beliefs of a particular Christian sector sets, accepts as a general basis for the good life those moral and ethical standards that have through the centuries been associated with what has come to be referred to in general terms as "the Christian way of life."

The differences in approach to the common problems besetting us all—as indeed in some measure is the case over defining exactly what is meant by "democracy" or the kind of cultural continuity considered most desirable—spring from the way in which the formulation of a political theory must take note of the character of the various social groups that together form the State: their purpose; their relative importance and size; causes of cohesion; the amount of control any given group is allowed to exercise over the individuals forming that group. This can perhaps best be instanced by a quick comparison of the differences in approach between the German and the English peoples.

In Germany the problem of achieving national unity

and a unification of the whole country has become for the German an historic task, still not realized and which must be courageously and vigilantly striven for. National unity came to Great Britain quite naturally and by a slow, logical procession of events extending from the Middle Ages onwards. With us there has been no real necessity for grim determination; and with us, in consequence, a policy of *laissez-faire* and of easygoing tolerance of all kinds of sub-groups within the main groups has resulted, leading to the foreigners' constant admiration of the Englishman's sense of "fair play" and almost comic perplexity at what he hears expounded by the soap-box orators in Hyde Park and elsewhere.

This in turn has influenced the general attitude towards the State. It is tradition in Germany, extending back in time to the eighteenth century, that the State should be strong and should make itself directly responsible for the welfare of its people. It has now become difficult for the modern German, conditioned as he is to consider himself under the guardianship and tutelage of the Stage, to see that he is the State and to assert fully his democratic rights as a citizen participating fully in the process of self-government. His interest in the State is as real as the Englishman's, but is passively patriotic whereas the Englishman's is critically attentive to the necessity for allowing each and every minority group its say—a process which naturally embraces the mixed blessings of local self-government and of decentralized local responsibility for education. In a word the Englishman's interest in the State machine is that of constantly weakening central authority and not of strengthening it, a process, of course, that is only possible when the question of national unity is once and for all settled beyond any possible doubt. So again is the attitude towards class structure influenced. In Great Britain this has always been rather loose: there has never been a caste system, and it has always been possible for the poor boy to rise by merit and ability to the highest and most important positions in the land. In Germany the policy of absolutism that was thought to be necessary in order the better to achieve national unity encouraged a rigid class structure—and such rigidity was subsequently found to be necessary for the perpetuation of the policy of absolutism. Finally, we should note that all these various factors have led in the case of Great Britain to the emergence of the idea that education is afforded as a means of permitting the individual to achieve personal significance, and to participate fully in the social and political life of his country. In Germany, education has been divorced from public life, and the middle classes, finding no place in the political activities of the strong State have been driven to achieve personal significance through a depending of their own experiences—through introspection. Thus, when as now happens the new techniques of scientific industrialism make their impact upon societies whose organization and habits of thought are adapted to an older system, making revolutionary challenges to the old ordered way of existence, the Germans—too rigidly cast in their would—feel inadequate and dread the future, an inescapable attitude of mind that is in direct contrast to the prevailing English philosophic balance that enables the Englishman to face the future calmly if vigilantly.

Insular security, of course, has been the chief factor in shaping and determining the characteristic philosophy and outlook of the British people. The insular situation has made political unity a possibility, a rich diversity of flourishing and unfettered sub-group culture that stimulate the whole nation a reality, a spirit of compromise over burning controversial questions inescapable, a rich common tradition that includes wide ranges of common experience, the mainspring of all action. In current jargon we tend to be amateurs who muddle through rather than planners with a clearly defined and undeviating purpose in view. We are at our best when improvising, and to improvise we draw on a lengthy tradition of self-discipline and voluntary co-operation. Unlike the introspective German, the Englishman finds his philosophy through action instead of determining his actions by the principles of philosophy. Formal instruction in the schools, therefore, has never been prized as highly as in France, or indeed Germany, and the discipline of experience has been constantly preferred to the discipline of school. For that reason we cannot make the clear distinction between "instruction" and "education" as do the French. We educate for personality rather than for literary attainment, and in terms of clearly understood social traditions in which the idea is implicit, as Ruskin put it, that "the character of men depends more on their occupation than on any teaching we can give them or principles we can imbue them with. The employment forms the habits of body and mind, and these are the constituents of man. Employment is the half, and the primal half of education." Or, as Sir Michael sadler has acutely observed on more than one occasion, just as apprenticeship was the keynote of medieval education in England, so does it remain the driving force behind educational practice to-day.

Nothing can make this point clearer than a close study of John Locke's *Thoughts Concerning Education* and of the influence it has had in moulding and shaping the pattern of a liberal middle class education throughout the last centuries—centuries during which the ideas of duty towards one's God, of duty towards one's neighbour, of working diligently"in that state of life unto which it shall please God to call me," firmly established themselves and made the State religion more a code of conduct than an act of faith; a resistance to any central unifying tendency on the part of the State an expression of a real belief in the efficacy of leaving as much as possible to individual responsibility and local self-government. It is for all these reasons that there is little likelihood of a uniform educational system ever appearing in Great Britain, and that any Education Act that is to prove acceptable throughout the whole country must be" a flexible stature leaving room for local and regional divergences... reflect our history and allow for the sensitivities that old conflicts have created."

Ultimately, of course, what is often regarded by foreign observers of the British way of life as an extremely individualistic conception of freedom and of social responsibility stems from a series of historical events that had a heightened significance for the island community they affected. Nowhere else in Europe in the thirteenth century could Magna Carta have been possible. The complete Protestant break from the power of the Holy See made inevitable a new kind of political nationalism and fostered the development of a mercantile economic society based on individual enterprise, The Civil Wars made clear to the new merchant bourgeoisie the importance of tolerance to the island community as a positive good and also as a vital necessity to the new" nation of shopkeepers," and also paved the way for the establishment of the present Parliamentary system of democratic government based on the restricted temporal and spiritual powers of Crown in Parliament.

In the attempt to achieve national unity, education in Germany has constantly been considered as a means of overcoming the individualistic stubborn tendencies of the peoples of the various *Lander* to weld these into *one* nation, *one* culture, *one* State, whilst yet allowing them to preserve as valuable forces for good their present individualistic characteristics. The doctrine of the strong *Land* that really cares for the welfare of its people, however, is still predominant and the problems which have fixed post-war Germany in preparing its people for a modern democratic way of life can only be judged in their correct magnitude when it is remembered that Germany, throughout its entire history from medieval to modern times, has been a democracy for roughly only fifteen years, and then more by compulsion than by spontaneous choice. In the case of Germany the Protestant Reformation did not produce democracy, mainly because Luther insisted on a rigid separation between the authority of the Church and the State and taught his Protestants not to interfere in political doctrine. In consequence the rulers of the various *Lander* built on the idea of a German religion for the German people based on strong autocratic, nationalistic and *Land* centred sentiments. Inevitably, then, education in Germany became little more than an end in itself, its only practical aim being that of the transformation of man into a worthy being whose life is determined by the desire for values. Hence the prevalence of the ideal of a "general education" which aims at developing a human being *not* primarily useful to the State, useful to society, or useful in his work, but one whose usefulness in different fields of activity is a consequence of his inner worth as a loyal member of his *Land* and of the German race. Even in the case of Kerschensteiner, a close examination of the programmes of work as laid down for the continuation school system of Munich will show this attitude of mind to be prevalent, if not immediately obvious.

Two outstanding names in modern French educational thought are undoubtedly those of Emile Durkheim, the sociologist, and "Alain," the philosopher and schoolmaster, and in their writings both illustrate quite plainly the prevailing and traditional outlook and approach. For Durkheim, education is a process of socialization by which each generation seeks to transfer its own traditions to its successor. "Education," he says, "is influence exercised by adult generations on those who are not yet mature for social life. Its aim is to develop in the child a certain number of physical, intellectual and moral qualities which are expected of him both by political society collectively and by the particular environment in which he is destined to live as an individual." Thus, according to his sociological method, education is an institution produced by society and the function of education in twentieth-century French society is to turn out men who conform to the ideal type of man envisaged by the society. Each individual pupil, therefore, is entitled to receive the sum of knowledge common to all, but no special consideration is shown for any particular individual as such. Alain, the teacher, gives the practical application of all this. He insists on wide but rapid reading for his pupils, and in the earlier years of books which, whilst they make an appeal to the imagination, contain some important underlying thought. Latin and geometry teach a child to think, and must be studied before anything else. The more austere the child's surroundings the better: he will think better. And education is an affair of thought, in the sense that the teacher thinks aloud and comments on a text in the pupils' presence with the object of stimulating in his pupils further thoughts of their own. Every thought should have a solid foundation of fact, for the natural way of learning is to proceed from the fact to the idea. To try to make things too easy for the pupil—to try to sugarcoat the pill to the extent that it is all sugar and no pill—is to do the pupil a great disservice. Alain in consequence looks askance at many of the ideas of the New Education, as he objects to observation lessons on the grounds that they "confine and paralyse the mind," The abstract and the general are much more accessible to the understanding of the child than natural objects which one cannot explain but which one can only dissect or observe. By the same token he deprecates attempts to explain modern theories which can only lead to a superficial knowledge of modern thought, and therefore a dangerous one.

As in the case of Germany, we have already had occasion to discuss at some length the influence of historical and political events on the shaping of the French national outlook. We can therefore content ourselves here with observing that the ideas expounded by Durkheim and Alain are based on the principle of claiming the absolute human value of the individual. If you know the truth you will act rightly. Then, society owes education to the child more for his own sake than for the advantages he will reap from threat education. The two important tasks of the school system are therefore (a) integration, and (b) the making of citizens. By "integration " is meant the maintenance of the moral and intellectual homogeneity of the whole nation, and towards this end it has been found that the Napoleonic system of centralization in the long run works best. The central authority recognizes best the general needs of the whole nation, and is thus best equipped for using the schools as an instrument for the assimilation of all sections of the population "ad maiorem Francorum gloriam." France educates for individual responsibility within the centralizing framework of the State; Great Britain educates for individual responsibility that makes the State; Germany educates for the strongly unified State.

The Belgian approach to the problems involved in educating for democracy is fundamentally not very dissimilar from the French, except that the Belgian's inherent love of liberty and his almost pathological need to be "up against authority" add more colour and diversity to the picture. Briefly, the attitude taken is that it is the responsibility of the State to provide a sound education for everybody and yet at the same time to sort out most carefully the elite capable of inspiring others by their example to great effort, and also of dealing intelligently and realistically with the increasingly complicated problems of modern existence as they particularly affect the destiny of a small State that becomes the pivotal point for any major European issue. It is firmly held that every healthy society needs its elite, and that false conceptions over equality of opportunity can dangerously lower standards both of intellectual attainment and also of national vitality. There is no reason, however, why this elite should be chosen from only one class.

The powers of the State are none the less most clearly defined. If it must see to it that all may benefit, and must dispense benefits impartially and justly it must in no sense dictate: "L'Etat ne cree pas; il encourage la crea:ion, controle et harmonise." Its job is primarily to organize for education, to intervene only when the interests of the whole State are imperiled, and therefore in general to ensure that there is a real respect for human personality, a genuine spirit of tolerance, a developing sense of civic pride, and a clear notion in men's minds of their duties towards their neighbour and towards the whole of humanity. The insistence on the State's peculiar function as a harmonizing influence also has its roots in past experience, and in particular in the nineteenth-century struggles between the Liberal and Catholic parties for the control of education. Just as it is conceded that the number of groups a person can belong to is bound to restrict his personal liberty in a variety of directions, so it is held that to belong to one group only can lead to enslavement to that group. The State's function, therefore, is to see to is that people are not subjected to the domination of one particular social group, but to make for as much diversity as possible within the general framework of government at both local and national levels. "Tout individuaest membre d'une clooectivite nationale envers laquelle il a des devoirs; mais il est aussi membre de plusieurs groupes sociaux particuliers; il est ou peut etre en outre un etre qui a sa fin en soi." It is interesting to note that since the passing of the 1944 Education Act and the creatioin of the Ministry of Education to replace the former Board of Education, the State machine in England has been moving gradually but surely in the direction of a centralization of effort that in many respects would not run counter to what would be approved in Belgian traditional practice.

The aims and aspirations of the Italian people have not much altered since they were first encouraged by

Napoleon to achieve national unity. It was grasped then, as surely as it is held now, that education must be the basis of the unified State. What is needed is a common culture that is not so much abstract and academic as concrete and living and in conformity with the soul of the people which it must revive to be successful in the task it sets itself. Education, therefore, must be universal and public—not necessarily the same for everyone, for it is important to sort out from the mass the elite required to guide the country's destiny and shape future policy. Education must also be uniform throughout the country because uniformity will ensure an easier control and provide a means for general supervision that alone can make for a satisfactory all-round level of attainment. It follows, therefore, that popular education must primarily be a function of the State, and the State cannot readily surrender this function without surrendering the most potent reasons for its existence. It is also to be remembered that in a country that is so predominantly Catholic, the pupil arrives in school with a mentality that has already been oriented in the Catholic direction. The school's task in consequence is to see to it that the forces already set in motion at the mother's knee are not vitiated or destroyed, but elaborated and broadened, once again in an attempt to quicken the soul of the nation as a whole. Religion in this sense ceases to be passive submission to an external authority and takes on a fuller and deeper significance, from the point of view of the State, as satisfying the most profound needs of the mind and therefore quickening the national pulse.

In direct contrast to Germany, the Scandinavian countries offer an example of how the Lutheran Reformation, and Protestantism generally, have been used in an attempt to achieve a real working democratic basis for government. We have noted earlier how the Lutheran idea of individual responsibility led in these Scandinavian countries towards the idea of a combined responsibility on the part of the State and Church for education, and how the close bonds between Church and State are still a marked feature of cultural life, thus bringing everybody during the most formative part of the educative process under the influence of the direct teaching of Christainity. When it is also remembered that in Sweden, since the days of Gustavus Adolphus, there have been two guiding principles at work—namely those of a strong State leadership, and of the recognition of education as an important factor in social development and therefore as an immediate objective for State activity—and that the Norwegian and Danish schools have been founded on the principles of freedom of beliefs, thought, and actions within a general framework of service to the community, it will be readily seen that the basic aim in these Scandinavian countries has been to produce a free, healthy-minded generation able to gain an independent outlook on the problems of their time; able to find their true place in society; realizing that they do not live alone in the world but must adapt their lives and actions to serve the good of the whole community from the family through to the nation and finally to all the peoples of the earth. Indeed, no better summing up of the dominant philosophical outlook of these countries can be found than that published as part of the text of the Norwegian teachers' declaration to their pupils issued on the 9th April, 1942, as a protest the attempted nazification of the schools:

We have been entrusted with the task of giving you

children that knowledge and training in thorough work which is necessary if you are to receive full and many-sided development as human beings, so that each one of you can take his or her place in the community for the benefit of himself and others. We have been given this calling by the Norwegian people, and the Norwegian people can call us to account for it. We also know that the sum total of knowledge and labour capacity which a country disposes of are the greatest and most durable of all its sources of wealth. It is our duty to protect those values...

The position in which Holland economically stands in relation to Europe and to the rest of the world has also made the problem of the interdependence of education and society a very real one, and it is recognized that sound educational policy must be based on concrete knowledge of the whole cultural position of the country. It was thanks to the Dutch Reformed Church that the Republic acquired a great number of schools within a short span, after liberation from Spanish domination, and it was also thanks to the Church—with its extremely democratic organization—that the schools took on from their earliest beginnings their peculiar democratic character that made for real national unity. When, by the Education Act 1806, the State stepped in to take over general control and to give the schools that national and systematically constructed system the various churches could not themselves provide, the general pattern of thought was already clearly defined. Toleration and a faith in man's ability to rise above himself to even greater efforts if he were given independence and full s cope in consequence to realize himself were becoming part of the "feelingtone" of the whole nation. Discrimination against Roman

Catholics and against others who stood outside the Reformed Church was eventually rejected and the parents' right to their own convictions in the bringing up of their children came scrupulously to be observed on the principle that national unity can never be attained by identifying one's own convictions with those of the nation: unity to be real and lasting must be based on a recognition of and a respect for variety. None the less the influence of Christianity is inescapably strong in the sense that the parents are still held to be the main if not the sole educators of their children. The Reformed Church was most careful to point out the tasks and responsibilities of parents in educating their children in accordance with the practice of their faith, and this parental sense of duty is today remarkably strong even amongst those who would claim the right to move completely outside the sphere of religious observances and practice. Education for national unity, then, is the aim behind the extremely democratic system that has been devised in Holland, it being at all times remembered that the active encouragement of sub-groups in all their diverse activities is a necessary concomitant. Unity out of diversity is the ideal.

We cannot end this analysis without reconsidering once again in some detail the aims of those two great countries that are so diametrically opposed in their views—the U.S.A. and the U.S.S.R. First of all, however, let us try to grasp as a whole and as pattern what is happening in the Western European democracies. In the most general terms, and with particular reference to the aims of secondary education, the late Sir Michael Sadler once wittily summed up the situation as follows: "The German is apt to ask about a young man, 'What does he know? 'The American to ask, 'What can he do? 'The

Frenchman to ask, 'What examinations has he passed? 'The Englishman's usual question is, 'What sort of a fellow is he? " In other word, the typical English attitude is one which distrusts intellectualism as such and which aims at producing a citizen type whose sense of justice, and loyalties and "fair play" is strong enough to make decentralization and local government based on individual enterprise and responsibility really work. The State is very much the servant and never the master of the individuals it purports to represent, and it is very much within the power of those individuals to exact from their elected representatives a detailed and exact account of their stewardship. In this sense, Great Britain stands very much apart from the rest of Western Europe—as much apart as does Western Germany, though for different reasons of which we have spoken earlier. The remaining democracies of Western Europe stress almost without exception the importance of there being "no better baggage on a journey than much of knowledge," Scandinavia and Holland falling very much under the spell of German intellectualism, France perpetuating the jesuit cult of scholarship for its own sake and for the intellectual discipline thereby afforded, and Italy rather more diffusely following a path parallel to that of the French but coming under the double influence of the Catholic Church and of the idealistic philosophy of Benedetto Croce. It is over the conception of the relationship of the individual to the State that the most noticeable differences occur, thus giving in each case a slight though important difference to the interpretation of what is meant by a democratic form of government, and thus causing subtle but important differences in the structure and administration of the educational machinery. These matters we shall discuss later.

The aim of Soviet education can be badly stated as being the propagation of Communism, in the process of which an elite of leaders for the various Soviets will be found and suitably trained along approved Marxist lines. "It is not the consciousness of human beings that determines their existence," wrote Karl Marx, "but, conversely, it is their social existence which determines their consciousness." In marxist doctrine a clear distinction must be drawn between society and the State. Society always exists, but the State is a more restricted organization within society, and it owes its rise to an inescapable dialectical conflict of class interests in which those who control the means of production oppress those who do not. The U.S.S.R. is seen as in a process of gradual evolution. At the moment private capitalism has been replaced by State capitalism. The ultimate goal is held to be this classless society, and in this important contemporary interim period it is the duty of each and every Russian tirelessly to equip himself, according to aptitude and ability, in order to help his country to move the more swiftly and expeditiously towards the goal. The practical and realist approach towards the pursuance of this ideal is typified by the avowed economic aim of outstripping the most advanced industrial countries in the world, and so freeing the Russian people for ever from the fear of want. Educational theory as such stresses the importance of the individual, insists constantly on the possibility for greatness that resides in the ordinary man, urges the release of that creative force which, it is claimed, resides in all human beings and which alone can bring them to the highest peak of human achievement that is necessary to form a truly classless society. Educational practice exacts a materialistic outlook, a stress on socially useful labour, an active participation from the pupils in the building and shaping of their own lives in terms of the Communistic ideal, and a close contact with contemporary life.

It may be argued that the Americans also lay great stress on active pupil participation in the building of their own lives, and on a close contact with contemporary life situations. It is certain that they are just as vocilerous as the Russians in claiming that they are educating for a true democracy. It is equally certain that despite the common language, their whole conception of the educative process is different from that holding in Great Britain, as their culture.and civilization are different. We have already seen how American character has been moulded by the necessity of constantly meeting the new situations which arose in the conquest of their frontiers. Resourcefulness and initiative are therefore qualities which the American most prizes in his fellow-countrymen, and a flexibility of mind that will seek successful adaptation to constantly changing circumstances. Thus, where the English stress the importance of character training as the end of education, the Americans emphasize training of the personality. Both countries, of course, seek to promote the fullest development of the individual, but whereas England has devoted the major part of its attention to the training of an elite, America has paid most attention to those pupils of average ability. As Professor Northrop has pointed out, it took one hundred and fifty years from the founding of the earliest colonies in New England for the idea of tolerance genuinely to establish itself in the new and growing continent, and that spirit of tolerance went eventually with Jefferson's belief that the common man would think and act rationally if allowed to do so, and that education's prime task was to give the common man the opportunity for proving himself in this direction all which means, as de Tocqueville pointed out, that the American, ultimately, is more interested in equality than in liberty. It is this individualistic egalitarian idea—"I'am as good as the next man!"—that leads to a kind of dramatization of the individual at all stages of development; that leads also, economically speaking, to the worship of success; that leads, ultimately, to the cult of the average man, which means conformity to the standards of the current majority. It also means that the American people are much more genuinely interested in their school system and what it can be made to do for their youngsters than are the peoples of any of the Western European democracies, though it must be remembered that the American tradition of local self-government has been an important factor in this direction. It finally means that America holds emphatically to the idea that the true aim of a democracy should be to adapt education to the ability and aptitude of each individual and to provide for each that education from which he is best able to profit. And America has discovered that a unitary planned system of education best achieves these objectives, and has, of course, a distinct initial advantage over most other countries in that its system has been unitary from the start.

All the other countries we have had under review have for a variety of reasons had nothing approaching such a unitary system, and their present attempts at offering each individual that education from which he and the country as az whole is best able to profit are made primarily on a basis of the traditional approach to which the country is accustomed, and are governed by the kind of system of educational administration the country enjoys.

The idea of the education of an elite is still prevalent in all countries, including the U.S.S.R. The Scandinavian countries come nearest to America in spirit, though Russia has adopted completely the unitary system. The English system has developed without any plan, new types of schools being added as the need arose, but without any articulation between them.

The administration of education

That the impact of the political theory of the State is most noticeable in the public supervision and administration of education will be readily understood when it is remembered that political theory must at some point define clearly the purposes of education and then go on to determine the type of administration which seems best suited to the attainment of the citizen type the State wishes to produce. It should, however, also be remembered that it was not until the eighteenth and nineteenth centuries that statesmen decided that universal and compulsory education was a desirable aim, and that even then they were more often than not inclined to leave the actual provision of the schools to someone else, usually the parishes and the local communities. When it became imperative that there should be some centralized control—if only for the reason that to make universal compulsory education a reality and not merely a law on the statute book the State must provide the necessary funds—then the kind of centralized control that was imposed had to take account of the prevailing culture pattern and of the aims and aspirations of the people as a whole as reflected so far in the organization of the school systems in vogue. Only in countries like Russia, or Germany and Italy under the Nazi and Fascist regimes, where a totalitarian system could be imposed, did it prove in any measure possible to impose a rigidly centralized administration to the exclusion of the participation of the public or any of its associated groups. And in the purely totalitarian state, of course, there can be no conflicting opinions and no criticism of theory and practice. Democracy for the Russians, considered from the educational point of view, means training in dialectical materialism and in socialism. Conformity to the Marxist ideal is the aim, and care is taken at all stages and at all levels to control all sources of information which may lead to "the harbouring of dangerous thoughts."

In consequence, the administration of education in Russia, though it is shared by several organizational, is in effect controlled entirely by the Council of People's Commissioners, by the Central Committee of the Communist Party, and by the Central Planning Commission of which each Minister for Education for each of the sixteen republics in the U.S.S.R. is a member. The Minister for Education thus takes part in deliberations and discussions on all national problems, thereby assuring a close and permanent link at the highest administrative level between education and the life of the Communist State. It is the responsibility of the Ministry of Education for each of the sixteen republics to see to the efficient organization of work in the primary and secondary schools, in the teacher-training colleges, in education bureaux, in education laboratories, in educational research institutes, and in the general sphere of adult education. True, there is some decentralization of administration in the sense that local bodies are required to maintain school buildings and approve the appointment of teachers, which is made by the head of the school, who is himself a Ministry nominee. They are also expected to take "an active interest" in the provision of facilities for the improvement of the efficiency of "in service" teachers and to provide adequate facilities for out-of-school activities. They can have no say, however, in the planning of the school syllabus, in the amount of time that shall be allotted to various subjects at various levels, nor in the approach to the teaching of the subjects on the curriculum, nor in the choice of textbooks.

Indeed, there are common or "stable" textbooks prescribed throughout the whole of the U.S.S.R. to ensure that the basic knowledge acquired is the same throughout the whole union, and that is consistently up to date in accordance with the latest high level pronouncements. There is also a common syllabus for the whole union, and a fixed timetable, to ensure that the main facts are taught to all children in the correct dosage. Apologists will often argue that much initiative is left to the local teacher to supplement all this as he will in accordance with local conditions and requirements, and that he is encouraged to draw on a wide variety of other material to supplement the textbook knowledge, the choice being entirely his. This is true...but he would be brave and rash man who attempted anything not in strict accordance with the party line and that was not going to win the immediate approval of the inspectorate!

Inspectors to the schools are appointed by each Ministry of Education, after some years of teaching experience during which they have proved themselves to be "sound." Their duties are many and their responsibilities considerable, their main task being that of constantly raising the standard of education and discipline in the schools and of co-operating closely with the head of the school to maintain the school's efficiency and reputation at the highest level. This means that they are constantly in and out of the school, listening to lessons and examining the work of the pupils. If an inspector considers that a lesson has been badly given, he will probably go over it in detail with the teacher in private, analysing it to show what was wrong, and then take the next lesson himself to show how it should be done. It is equally the inspector's duty, together with the head of the school, to recommended a teacher for an award or promotion. Finally, in order to ensure that the inspectors themselves do not in any sense deviate from the party line, and are kept constantly informed of the various shifts and emphasis that are from time to time required, there is an institute for the training of inspectors, this training being followed up by regular refresher courses held every three months. As one Russian university professor once put it: "Our education sets itself the task of creating all-round, active, determined possessors of knowledge and of the proletarian world outlook, devoted to communism and communistic morality, builders and defenders of a socialist society." There could be no more direct and simple statement of a completely totalitarian aim.

Of course, several of Western European democracies—notable amongst which are France, Belgium, Sweden and Holland—enjoy or have enjoyed in varying degrees the mixed blessings of a highly centralized system in many respects not dissimilar from that holding in the U.S.S.R. But there comparison stops short, for the ends to be served in these countries by a policy of centralized control of education are neither political nor ideological, but rather based on a definite theory of education that seems best to suit the peculiar requirements of the country in the light of its past endeavours and achievements. Again whilst the character of the administrative may be authoritarian, authority and controls are limited to the actual work done in the schools and to providing a uniform school system, and are in no sense extended to cover the private lives of teachers, parents, pupils and citizens generally outside the school. A parent or teacher may hold whatever political or religious views he pleases, may freely criticize both the theory and practice of education, and—if he does not like what is provided for him by the State—may send his children to a private "free" school or start such a school himself, subject only to general governmental regulations covering adequacy of buildings and equipment and the employment of suitably qualified teachers, the qualifications exacted from teachers in the "free" schools being by no means necessarily as high as those required for employment under State control. Broadly speaking, such countries among the democracies as to-day have some form of centralization use their powers to make certain that the pupils in the schools have acquired both a certain body of knowledge and a mind trained to think for itself. Again, we must remember that without direct intervention on the part of the State the organization and provision of adequate educational facilities for all children would have been impossible in Holland, Belgium and Scandinavia, just as it was proving impossible in England until the passing of the 1944 Education Act which itself proved a step towards a more authoritarian and centralized control.

The advantages that are usually claimed for the centralized system are that opportunities are equalized, and that the rural and more remote areas have as good educational facilities as the more advanced and progressive urban areas; that the quality of education provided is uniform because all schools are provided with teachers possessing the same qualifications; and that the system is efficient because the same standards are set for all schools. This, of course, is only true to a point. All teachers are not of equal calibre even if they have all followed identical courses and passed the same examinations. Nor, in actual practice, do we find the more able and more ambitious teachers willing to bury themselves in remote country areas. Nor, finally, do examination successes show that the same standards of achievement have been achieved in different schools of the same system. A more serious criticism of the tightly centralized system, however, is that local initiative and enterprise is stifled and there is no real incentive to the sub-groups seriously to challenge accepted because practised doctrines. The real vigour of the English educational system has lain in the wide diversity and variety of aims and purposes that have only been made possible through a policy of complete decentralization. The stagnation that has repeatedly been complained of in experimentation in aims and methods in French schools was the inevitable outcome of a strongly centralized system, dating from the 1880's, that virtually nil. It is interesting to note that post-war reforms in English education to be effective have had to initiate a closer control of local responsibility and private enterprise, whereas in France there has had to be a relaxation of control in order to allow what was considered desirable experimentation to take place.

What is obviously wanted in those countries which still believe in the importance to the country as a whole of the formation of an intellectual elite is a careful distribution of functions between the central and the local authorities and achieves real liberty with a high degree of conformity, and it is the proud and justifiable boast of the Dutch that they have managed to do this. The inevitable struggle between Church and State for the control of education led to a series of uneasy compromises in the predominantly Catholic countries, but generally speaking these countries—in particular France and Belgium—achieved a working solution to the problems facing them on a basis of what we might call "liberty without the State system." That is to say, the State has undertaken the maintenance and development of a neutral system of education open to all who care to profit by it. Those sections of the community who are for one reason or another dissatisfied with what the State offers may, if they so wish, establish side by side with the State schools "free" schools which become their entire responsibility. In principle the State adopts a passive attitude towards such schools. There is, however, another solution which might be termed "liberty within the State system," and it is this solution the Dutch have sought. Passivity is replaced by active State intervention. Thus the State actively assist the development of such schools as are not neutral, provided certain guarantees are given that the instruction in those schools will be equivalent to, though not necessarily identical with, that given in the neutral schools. Since 1945 both France and Belgium have felt compelled to treat the Catholic "free" schools in their respective countries on not dissimilar lines by granting State subsidies proportionate to those voted for the State schools towards their upkeep and general maintenance.

Alongside all this, however, Holland has devised her own peculiar form of decentralization. Though the Ministry of Education supervises the whole system it most definitely does not act as "schoolmaster-in-chief." Its function is to achieve uniformity of standards and of educational opportunity throughout the country; to pay the salaries of all approved teachers in whatever school they serve, to regulate the execution of the programme of studies and the timetable of lessons, to see that regulations effecting efficiency in schools are complied with, to see to it that any group of persons legally in a position to demand the establishment of a "free" school are not denied their rights, and to make a large contribution towards the upkeep of the secondary schools proper. To enable it efficiently to carry out these various duties, the Ministry has an inspectorate consisting of three chief inspectors and fifty-six others assigned to different districts. There are two architect-inspectors in addition whose sole concern is school buildings, and two inspectors or teacher-training.

The immediate responsibility for the provision of adequate primary, secondary and technical education falls on the local authorities, the public schools being managed by the municipal council and a board consisting of bungomaster and aldermen, the "free" schools being privately managed but he local authority being held responsible for supplying the necessary school buildings. The local authorities appoint local inspection committees on which parents, teachers and other local citizens are represented. To sum up, the local authorities pay all current expenses and provide the buildings for all types of schools, the Ministry pays all salaries and in addition makes adequate grants towards the efficient maintenance of good secondary education. About 27 per cent of the children attend neutral State primary schools, about 28 per cent attend "free" Protestant schools, about 43 per cent. attend "free" Roman Catholic schools, and 2 per cent.

only are in neutral "free" schools—that is to say, schools which belong to no religious body and which equally wish to remain "free" from municipal control. The Dutch love of freedom and independence which probably found its greatest expression for all time in the eighty years' struggle ceaselessly waged to secure freedom from the Spanish yoke finds in modern times its fullest expression in this present system which harmoniously combines the benefits of both a centralized and a decentralized system of educational administration.

The situation holding in France is radically different from that in Holland, the local authorities having in effect no say in the policy to be adopted, their functions being restricted in the main to the supply of furnishings, heating, lighting, and so on, and even then being very carefully guided by some specific regulation as to exactly how and when and why and in what measure they shall act. All authority is exercised by the Minister for Education, under the control of Parliament, and by his delegates in each of the twenty-six *academies* into which the country is administratively divided. At the head of each *academie* is the *Recteur*, appointed by the President of the Republic and directly responsible to the Minister. Usually he is chosen from among the university professors, but the only qualification he actually needs is the possession of a doctorate degree. The *Recteur* has almost absolute powers within his *academie*, and he directs the whole system of education from the nursery school upwards to the university, and including the general supervision of all private schools. His administrative assistants include, since the last war, an inspector general for primary education, one for youth and sports, and one or more for technical education. Under his control, and representing both the

Recteur and the Minister, is an academy inspector for each of the *departments* contained within the *Academie*. This academy inspector controls his team of inspectors who are specialists chosen to cover all types of education offered within any given *department*. It should be noted that there is in addition a *departemental* council that fulfils in each *department* the important role of administering the whole of primary education; and in particular holds itself responsible for the recruitment, training and promotion of primary school teachers. This is a traditional arrangement, extending back to the first attempt at organizing primary education in France and when the Minister of the Interior, through his *prefets*, sought on orderly solution.

At the highest level the Minister and his numerous advisers an assisted by a body of special inspectors of national education whose function it is to visit all educational establishments, to report on the teachers therein, to keep the Minister constantly informed of the over-all picture of education throughout France, and—most important of all in many ways—to plan the programme of studies for the schools, to think out new lines of approach in view of constantly changing conditions, and to indicate quite clearly and dogmatically what are, in the Ministry's view, the best methods of instruction to be adopted. All these inspectors are, of course, specialists in one given branch, though they may from time to time be charged with a job of work that extends beyond the confines of their speciality. Since 1946 this rigid top-level structure has been to some extent modified by the formation of various new consultative committees on which the actual teaching personnel are represented, and by widening the representation in the teachers' favour on the important *Counceils d'Enseignement* and *Counseil Superieur* which are concerned with all projects of reform of education. Further, there has been a marked tendency over the last twenty years or so to permit local divergences from the fixed programme of studies, particularly in the last year of the primary school, in technical education, and in advanced and specialized work at the university level or its equivalent.

A further peculiarity of the French system, and one still further accentuating the strongly centralized approach, is that all examinations without exception are State examinations, and not merely school leaving examinations conducted in part or as a whole by the school authorities concerned with the pupil. Any child, provided he fulfils the necessary age qualifications may present himself anywhere for examination in the appropriate subjects, it making no difference whether he has been privately educated at home, ar in a State a "free" school. Private "free" establishments can, of course, issue their own diplomas, but they have no value whatever in securing one of the innumerable appointments which always specify success in one or a number of State examinations. Naturally, the obligation on everybody to present themselves for the State examinations ensures that the programme of work in all "free" establishments will be the same as in the State schools and that the approach to the teaching of the various subjects will not greater differ. Finally, there is the *concours* or competitive examination where the number accepted does not only depend on the high quality of work achieved but also on the number of placed valuable—for example, the *concours d'agregation* for teachers at a secondary and university level.

This principle of the centralization of education was

first enunciated by La Chalotais in 1763, upheld by the writers of the French Revolution, and cast in its final practical mould by Napoleon in 1808. And Napoleon quite consciously imitated many of the features of the organization of the Society of Jesus that over the preceding centuries had done so much to create an intellectual elite as a basis for a strongly centralized monarchial regime. As he himself put it, he was anxious to secure for the State all the advantages that were obviously secured for the Church of Rome by the Jesuit organization, an dot secure a class of civil servant who would have not other ambition except to be useful, and no other interest except public welfare. "My aim in establishing an educational corporation is to be able to direct political and moral opinions." Not unnaturally we find that, since France was by this time the spiritual leader of the Latin world, most of these Latin countries followed the model set then by Napoleon for the organization of their educational systems.

The centralization of administration was introduced as far as the kingdom of Sardinia was concerned well before the Napoleonic reforms. Napoleon's conquest of the Northern Provinces led to their incorporation in the French Empire, and in the south of Italy Joseph Bonaparate and Murat were naturally bound to pursue a policy of close centralization on the approved French model, particularly so when it is remembered that Napoleon owed the germ of his idea for centralization from what he had seen operative in the kingdom of Sardinia. With the founding of the Ministry of Public Instruction in Italy and the passing of the Casati Law of 1859, centralization had been extended to all the provinces, and the Casati Law itself, again following

French practice, left primary education to the initiate of the local authorities and maintained only the secondary and higher schools. Under the Fascist regime Gentile was instrumental in reducing the sixty-nine provinces into nineteen regions that each had their own historical frontiers and in furthering "regional" activities and so allowing each historical region to vary its curricula to suit local bias, local traditions and peculiar outlook. Further, the neutral State schools have never been neutral in the French sense that no religious teaching of any kind shall be done there. It is also to be noted that various attempts abortive, and that, mainly for financial reasons, the country as a whole would now seem to prefer the centralized system.

Supreme over all education in Italy is the Minister, assisted by an under-secretary with an educational cabinet of his own. Eight director-generals of education are in charge of general affairs and of personnel, and amongst them cover the whole field of education including university and higher education, antiquity and fine arts, academies and libraries and cultural relations. The highest authority in a province is the Chief Inspector of Studies, who is directly responsible for all matters concerning primary education and who also supervises the secondary schools. The actual task of school visitation, inspection and supervision is carried out by a team of school inspectors. The Chief Inspector of Studies also appoints a provincial school council consisting of an expert in primary education, a professor, a teacher, a physician and the chief engineer for public works. Thus council provides the Chief Inspector with all the technical advice he needs and under his chairmanship deal with questions of school organization, including finance and staffing. The Chief

Inspector of Studies is a Ministry nominee and representative.

The slight but important divergences from the French system that have appeared indicate the Italian's historical consciousness of regional differences, reflect and betrary a marked Germanic influence and strong Catholic outlook. In the case of Belgium, with its own peculiar stormy history, its strong Catholic and non-Catholic parties, and the linguistic problems presented by the Flemings and the Walloons, there are many differences to be noted. By population and tradition, Belgium of course is not a typical Latin country, and the old system of local and provincial self-government is very much in evidence despite the centralized system that is imposed for the sake of uniformity. According to the usual pattern, there is a Minister with his boards of advisers and a ministerial inspectorate with very wide powers of supervision in that they control material organization, curricula, pedagogical methods, and enforce a strict execution of the law as centrally interpreted. When by the law of 1932 Belgium was officially divided into Flemish and Walloon areas, so was the inspectorate divided, though each separate body was subordinated to the control of the Ministry. Whilst it is generally true to say that-secondary and higher education is administered directly by the Ministry, and that primary education is left as a responsibility of the local authorities and the provinces, it must be remembered that several large towns and provinces still cling jealously to their independence, insist on controlling their own secondary schools, and strive often to keep ahead of rival institutions in other towns and provinces in their ability to recruit the best possible teaching staff and to make use of the best and most modern school equipment available.

There are in all ten provinces, each with a governor chosen by the King, each with a provincial council elected by popular vote. Similarly, there is in each commune a communal council the executive head of which is the burgomaster assisted by any number of from two to six *echevins* selected by ballot from the rest of the members of the council. Amongst these *echevins* one is responsible for educational matters within the commune.

It is, of course, the boast of the Belgians that in accordance with their constitution all education is free in the sense that anybody can open a school. Education generally, however, is of two types: either "free" or Roman Catholic, or State and therefore secular. School figures to-day indicate that the children are roughly divided between the two types of school, there being quite a number of Catholics attending the State schools. The Belgian insistence on the liberty of the subject is further exemplified by the fact that in the State secular schools two hours per week are left open for religious or moral instruction. According to the wishes of the parents, a priest of the appropriate denomination will attend to give this instruction. Where parents do not wish for this, then the children follow a course of moral instruction given by an appropriate teacher. Again, at the level of higher education, the State provides two State universities, one at Ghent for the Flemish-speaking population, one at Liege for the Walloons whose language is French. The Catholics, however, have their own "free" university at Louvain, and a secular "free" university is established in Brussels. Finally, the Catholic schools have established their right to their own body of inspectors, who naturally follow the main directiveness laid down by the Ministry.

Further flexibility in the system is to be found in that

each secondary school has its own leaving examination, the only State interference being through a *Jury d'Homologation* whose job it is, acting in a general supervisory capacity, to ensure that a certain level of attainment is reached—in other words that the national standards are maintained in all schools. Thus there is nothing as impersonal as the *baccalaureat* in France, and no State system of examinations as such—though the system of *concours* is in existence in certain specialized fields though not in effect in teaching.

It is significant to note that a decentralized system of administration developed almost entirely amongst peoples of Germanic origin or tradition where for one reason or another the Roman legal system did not take deep roots and therefore could not supersede the old customs of self-government. The efforts of the monarchy to achieve a strongly centralized State could not wear down the sturdy opposition of the aristocracy and of the people. And the Reformation further rendered abortive such efforts at centralization as persisted by the organization of the Protestant churches on the basis of a self-governing parish. Whatever centralization was later achieved was willingly conceded by the people as a whole in the interests of national uniformity, though care was none the less taken to preserve the administrative independence of the local authorities. We have already seen how this has worked out in practice in both Holland and Belgium. We must now examine in some detail the systems of more typically decentralized countries such as Germany, the Scandinavian countries, Switzerland, and of course England.

Germany is in many ways untypical in that the decentralization takes the form of allegiance to the *Land* rather than to a local authority, and the *Land* can often be extremely authoritarian in the control it exercises. The Thirty Years War left the various *Lander* divided amongst themselves and Germany as a whole in a state of political disintegration. As a result the individual *Land*, and not the *Reich*, assumed control of the schools and determined their form and organization, and each *Land* continued to hold and exercise this function until the Weimar Constitution was adopted after the First World War. Articles in this constitution determined a basis for a common school legislation, but nothing was done to implement this, and the *Lander* continued, in the field of education at any rate, to retain complete autonomy. A slight step towards uniformity was taken by agreements negotiated between several *Lander*, when conformity over general standards of education was established. The National introduced further measures to bring about unification, and created in 1934 the Reich Ministry of Education.

The overwhelming difficulties that faced the Germans on the collapse of the Nazi regime, and the complications involved in having to contend with four separate occupying Powers, led once more to the various *Lander* retaining control of school legislation and administration. This time, however, the various Ministers of Education, sensing the need for co-operation between the various *Lander* if the new democratic principles involving a unified Germany were to be realized, formed themselves into a permanent conference which, working quietly and efficiently over post-war years, has done much towards achieving a uniform purpose in education for the whole country. Thus, general agreement has been achieved on: the adoption of grades of equal value and formulation to be used on school reports and certificates; the introduction of optional foreign language instruction in the primary school; principles of political education in school; adoption of uniform principles of spelling; mutual recognition of certificates of maturity entitling admission to the universities; the methods of professional preparation of secondary school teachers; the standardization of school holidays. None the less, much still be done before the ideal of real harmony in German education is achieved.

Within each *Land* there are three level of administration: the State Ministry of Education; the Government-District; and the country level, which is either rural or urban. General school policy, curriculum planning, the setting up of examination requirements, the final certification and appointment of teachers, ar all handled at the ministerial level. The Government-District and the county levels of administration have functions of local administration and supervision, the supervision of the secondary schools being separate from that of the primary schools and attaching to the Ministry. Both these school authorities, however, receive their directions from the Ministry, and any innovations they may wish to introduce must first of all have ministerial sanction. They are, on the other hand, held responsible for seeing that school regulations in the primary schools and in the intermediate schools are scrupulously observed, for guiding and advising teachers, for the in-service training of young teachers, and for the licensing of private teachers, including those who wish to "tutor" pupils who need or seek special assistance.

As in Belgium, the *Abitur* examination is a more informal and "homely" affair than in France, the teachers in the schools setting the examinations the senior inspector for the *Land* vetting the questions before they are actually put and having the right of choosing among a number or changing them, and always taking part in the important viva voce section of the examination as chairman of the examining panel.

Thus in this modern attempt to proceed along real democratic lines the German people have recognized the right of the member-states of the Federal Republic to preserve their won particular features of education, and the individual states, in their turn, have devised a working machinery in the Permanent Conference of Ministers of Education for reaching compromises between the administrations of the individual states for the benefit of the cultural way of life of all of them. Diversity, which in the past has so largely contributed to the riches of German cultural life, is maintained; but harmony is encouraged in order to facilitate transfers from the schools of one *Land* to those of another. The goal is not complete uniformity of education throughout the Federal Republic, but equivalent based on a centralized *Land* system.

In many ways Switzerland might be considered purely from the point of view of education administration, as "Germany writ small." The country is divided into twenty-five independent *cantons*, and within these *cantons* there are about three thousand more or less autonomous political communities, each having considerable jurisdictional authority. Education is consequently the joint affair of the *Bund*, of the *canton*, and of the local community; there is no Ministry of Education, but complete delegation of responsibility to local authorities who have, incidentally, always to consider that there are four official nation languages for the whole of Switzerland. As in Germany, the *Bund* places the responsibility on the *cantons* for seeing to it that education is free, adequate, compulsory and without religious discrimination." No attempt is made in the Constitution to define what is meant by "adequate education." The *canton* feel that education is not adequate he is free to appeal to the *Bund* to seek redress. "Compulsory education" means that the *canton* is responsible for seeing that sufficient instruction is received according to local *cantonal* regulations, but not that children shall attend a State school. All schools, however, whether private or public, must achieve a minimum standard of instruction, and *cantonal* inspectors have supervisory control over the curriculum of both private and public schools. At State primary schools and many of the secondary schools are administered directly by the local communities, and the teachers are appointed locally. The local community also maintains the schools and pays teachers' salaries, though the *cantons* lay down compulsory scales of pay and grant subsidies to their local communities. The Federal Government subsidises teachers' salaries, buildings, welfare work and the preparation of teachers for the primary schools. It also pays about half the cost of vocational training and supervises this.

Obviously the Swiss Republic is the only country is Europe where the old system of extreme decentralization has remained practically unchanged. And equally obviously the Swiss have proved that a really high standard of educational endeavour and achievement can be obtained with such a system, rivalling in all spheres the best in all other countries. Differences of language, religion and cultural traditions, dependent in turn on the geographical configuration of the country, account for the perpetuation of an extreme form of decentralization. Economic circumstances have forced the Swiss to demand a high standard of education from all and for all. Historical events have led to a real spirit of democracy among the people, and this in turn has led to a stressing of the importance of education as a means of producing the good citizen type who will be a well-informed and progressive member of the community.

The Scandinavian countries are constitutional monarchies in which the functions of the Crown are analogous to those of the Crown in Great Britain. The controlling power of government is vested in the people who elect their parliamentary bodies on a principal of universal suffrage. The dissemination of culture is wide, and all classes of people play an active part in community and national life. Characteristic also of these countries is that private capitalism and social collectivism are co-extensive. In Sweden, for example, all public utility services are the concern of either the State of the logical government—yet almost all industrial workers are privately employed. Throughout Scandinavia generally the whole of the arable land is privately owned and tilled—and yet the farmers form themselves into co-operative societies to market their productive. Finally, it should be noted that the "welfare state" has been long the concern of these countries as a means of achieving real economic and social stability. Education has been deliberately used throughout the centuries to bring about this high degree of voluntary collectivism, and public education as part of the urge towards popular enlightenment that came with the Reformation has been a national concern since the sixteenth century.

The administration of education, originally in the hands of the Lutheran Church and of local boards, has now become a joint concern of both the State and the local communities. In Norway there is still a "Ministry of Church and Education" which is responsible for all supervision of education, and which for this purpose has a staff of consultants and travelling inspectors for special subjects. The Norwegian "People's School" is run by the local authority, is governorship being the direct responsibility of the people. In every municipality that there is a school board appointed by the elected municipal council but which must contain a clergyman of the State Church nominated by the bishop, and a teacher nominated by his own colleagues. This school board is held responsible for the local school administration in compliance with the existing laws of the country. The school board appoints its own teachers, subject to ratification of the appointment by the Ministry. Usually it secures the services of a local school inspector to supervise the administrative as well as the pedagogic side of the school work.

An over-all control of primary education is maintained by the Ministry which divides the country into seven administrative districts at the head of each of which is a school director. Any differences of opinion within the school boards, or between the school boards and the directors, may be referred to the Ministry for a final decision. The secondary schools originated from schools opened at the bishops' sees from 1150 onwards, and even to-day still bear in most cases the stamp of their ecclesiastical origins. These schools can be either State or municipally controlled. A State secondary school has a board of governors consisting of the headmaster, a representative of the Ministry, one representative of the teaching staff, and from one to four members of the local authorities in whose district the school is situated. The school boards act as governors for the municipally controlled schools. The final school-leaving examination is the same throughout the country and is organized by a special council of secondary education, the members of which are nominated by the King for a period of five years, and who inspect the schools and act as advisers to the Ministry. The total expenditure on education is roughly divided equally between the local authority and the State.

With only slight, and from our point of view unimportant variations, the same administrative pattern holds for both Sweden and Denmark. One interesting feature in Denmark, however, is that if the parents so desire they may establish a parents' council which shall have the power of school inspection and which may assist the Board of Education and in the selection of teachers—this for primary schools only, appointments of staff and general supervision of the secondary schools being the direct concern of the Ministry.

One interesting feature which all these countries so far under discussion share in common is that—no matter whether the administration of education be centralized or decentralized—they have as their aim the formation of an intellectual elite, and they believe strongly in the advantages that can be gained from a strictly academic type of secondary education. As a result, education at the secondary level is generally considered far too important a concern to be left too much in the hands of the local authorities, and the State has increasingly made this type of education its special concern. The contrary can be said to hold in both England and the United States. On the other hand, the chief difficulty in both England and the United States, because of the persistence of their own peculiar traditions traditions of local control of education, is that of implementing the ideal of equality of educational opportunity. All the other countries, centralized or decentralized as their administration may be, are meeting with relatively greater success. It would seem that the most likely explanation for this is that education in these other countries has always been held to be an important instrument in securing the people's allegiance to a particular form of government and to a particular way of life that on its showing made the people in turn happy, prosperous, and therefore contended. Thus in Scandinavia the decentralized system was imposed on the people by a Lutheran Church which seriously held that Christian salvation came through enlightenment of the people and that the only way to work at the people's level was through the smaller parish community. In France a highly centralized system was imposed *ad maiorem Francorum gloriam*, the hierarchical system of the Catholic Church, and in particular of the Jesuit Order, being the obvious model to follow-as indeed in all predominantly Catholic countries Russia—the only country to adopt the American unitary system of education—makes it work much more effectively through a form of centralization and through gearing it to the Marxist ideal. Holland and Belgium are in the midway position between extremes of centralization and decentralization, with State control acting as a "harmonizing" influence, and the Germans are hoping to move increasingly towards this.

England and America, each in their own particular sphere, have manifested a widespread opposition to uniformity and educational prescriptions of any kind. In both countries there is strong feeling against delegating the control of education to a central national authority, an equally strong belief in local control as a method of stimulating voluntary effort on the part of the community. None the less, both countries have had to realize that the extreme form of decentralization they have enjoyed has in the long run militated against securing equality of opportunity, and have had to make definite moves towards some further form of centralization to harmonize over-all endeavour. Little more than twenty years ago there existed in the United States 40,605 separate local administrative bodies for education, with more members on the boards of education in some States than there were teachers and ranging in size from localities with a single teacher school to a system like that of New York City with about 36,000 teachers. In England there were no fewer than 315 local education authorities, some very progressive, some extremely backward. England has now managed to reduce this number of local authorities to 163, and the number of local boards in the United States is being rapidly diminished. In England also, the Education Act of 1944, replacing the old Board of Education by a Ministry of Education, has given greater powers of determining policy to this Ministry which has in turn assumed a larger share in the financial support of education. Over the last thirty years or so moves have been constantly made to secure a greater participation by the Federal Government in the provision of funds for education, but—apart from funds for various special types of education, mainly vocational—any attempts through Federal aid to equalize education opportunities or to establish reasonable standards throughout the whole country have been resisted through fear of Federal control. The fundamental problems for both England and the United States are thus those of how to increase funds for education from the national purse without interfering with the rights of local authorities to adapt education to local or regional needs, and how also to maintain satisfactory standards of education uniformity throughout the country.

If the American Federal Government has played virtually no part in education, neither can the State governments themselves be said to be in a position to exercise the same control within each state that is exercised by the *Land* within Germany, for example. Within each state there is a Board of Education responsible to the legislative power for issuing general directives and programmes of education for the training of teachers, and for meeting roughly 50 per cent. of the total cost of education. The rest of the money has to be found by the separate L.E.A.'s which vary greatly in size, population wealth and efficiency. It is, therefore, the L.E.A. that determines more particularly the actual programme of studies and decides that salaries are to be paid, the local costs for education being met out of the local rates and taxes on a special budget. This is the direct result of the Jefferson championing of democracy which, it will be remembered, argued that education was a function of government—of local self-government. In a word the Jeffersonian approach means that the history of education in the United States is the history of the education of the public itself, and that progress must depend on he ability of the general public to realize education's value and significance. Hence the emphasis, in all local communities, on education weeks, press publicity, school demonstrations, public education meetings, school exhibitions, parent-teacher associations. Education must kept constantly in the public eye. The taxpayer must know that he is getting value for his money, and a healthy rivalry must be fostered between neighbouring communities both to stir the sluggish and to lead to further experimentation. More recently, as the disadvantages under which the smaller and poorer communities have to work have been more acutely realized, these have been encouraged to pool their resources and built a common school to which children may travel from the more distant parts by bus. Where there is not adequate high school accommodation, arrangements are being increasingly made with the nearest authority capable and willing to absorb an extra population, to take the high school children of the "foreign" L.E.A. on a *per capita* basis of payment. Over the whole of this the Federal Office of Education in Washington keeps an approving eye and confines itself in the main to carrying on the job it was assigned when first created in 1867: that of collecting and diffusing such statistics and facts are calculated generally to promote the cause of education throughout the U.S.A.

The central authority education in England and Wales is the Ministry of Education, with a politically chosen Minister who has a seat in the Cabinet, and a stall of permanent civil servants divided into two groups: those who serve at the administrative central headquarters, and those who act as inspectors and who are assigned to areas administered by local authorities. The Ministry does not maintain, provide, or directly control any kind of educational institution, but through its inspectorate it none the less exercises considerable influence. The work of the inspectors—who are servants of the Crown and not of the Minister—falls into three clearly defined areas: that of inspecting school, consulting with local authorities and teachers and giving advice where necessary; that of representing the Minister in their local areas on administrative matters; and that of advising the Minister in matters of educational theory and practice and of being responsible for the Ministry's publications. Prior to the passing of the Education Act of 1944 only state-aided schools were subject to inspection; under the terms of the Act *all* schools without exception must be open to inspection and must conform to minimum requirements as laid down by the Ministry.

The function of the L.E.A.'s is to provide a full range of educational opportunity at the primary, secondary, technical and further education levels, and they are responsible to the Ministry for the proper conduct of the schools they establish. Just as each L.E.A. in the United States has its superintendent of schools, so in England there is the chief officer. The important difference between the United States and England, however, is over the matter of finance: fully two-thirds of the total expenditure on education in each I.E.A. in England comes from national funds; in the United States the Federal Office of Education has until recently contributed almost nil, the local state boards up to 50 per cent., the L.E.A. meeting the remainder.

It is in many ways an interesting object lesson for the Americans to note that, despite the large sums devoted to education from the State funds in England, the L.E.A. still remains considerable independence of action. On the other hand, the Education Act of 1944 brought England much closer to European practice by replacing the former former President of the Board of Education by a Minister and a Ministry of Education, and by giving the Minister much more positive functions. In addition to inspecting and allocating grants the Minister is further enjoined to "promote the education of the people of England and Wales." He can compel the L.E.A.'s when necessary and advisable to adopt a definite line of policy. And the Act itself, in order to iron but glaring inconsistencies, actually commanded local authorities to provide facilities—such as nursery school accommodation and schools for handicapped children—that had not formerly been readily available. It is unlikely, however, that there will be any significant further move towards more compete centralization. The peculiar English traditions of local government and of voluntary service at that level are too firmly entrenched.

5
Autonomy Support in Education

Schools represent the most important context in middle childhood and adolescence for this development of autonomy. Through education a child presumably acquires competencies and skills which make possible later economic and social adaptation. However, perhaps more significant than skills *per se* is the growth of the motivation and interest in exercising, elaborating, and applying them. Stated differently, successful education breeds more than technical competence; it deepens an individual's confidence and sense of agency, which is so essential to self-direction and self-respect as an adult. This is the affective aspect or goal of education: to facilitate the personality development of children in a direction of greater motivation and independence in the processing of learning, achievement and social relatedness. Yet on the topic of this affective component of education many educational theorists are notably mute.

Movement away from the absolute dependence of early infancy and toward the relative independence of adulthood is the universal path along which all persons must travel. Most developmental psychologists and educators assume that there are natural or inherent tendencies that can be found in every child, which lead him or her in the direction decreased heteronomy and greater self-direction. However, once that is assumed, the *practical* question remains of identifying and creating those condition which facilitate rather than forestall this process.

The purpose of the present chapter is to focus on this more enigmatic aspect of educational practice. Our task is to examine the role of teachers and parents in facilitating the development of autonomy and self-regulation in children. To do so we will call upon a variety of research and field studies in the academic context. It will be argued that only through a classroom and school community context which supports the exercise of autonomy is the child likely to grow to identify with the values of that community and what is has to offer. Further, only insofar as autonomy and self-regulation are fostered will praise and esteem for actions be adequately internalized as 'self'-esteem, and therefore contribute to confidence and self-direction in adulthood.

Many people become wary .when it is suggested that autonomy he promoted. They suspect something uncivilized or chaotic will emerge when autonomy is advanced. Thus, rather than support and guide the natural trend toward autonomy, they instead battle with nature. Autonomy in this view is something to be curtailed, shaped, or controlled lest it conflict with pre-ordained values. Yet such a view neglects the fact that autonomy does not mean the absence of values; it means instead learning to identify with and independently exercise them. Summarily, autonomy does not mean escape from work or achievement. Rather it means the acquisition of an interest and sense of importance for the activity of one's work, and thus of self-motivation and choice within it. Autonomy does not mean the neglect of all discipline; it means growing away from dependence on external controls toward self-regulation and self-management.

Reciprocally, the promotion of autonomy involves not an avoidance of activity on the part of a teacher or parent but rather great subtlety and expertise. Autonomy develops and is strengthened only insofar as it is exercised, and eliciting that exercise requires skilled and creative practice. One cannot push someone to be self-directed without unwittingly undermining that goal. Similarly, one cannot teach another to be responsible without first giving over some responsibility. In this sense, autonomy promotion is a facilitative rather than a training process. It requires attending to the internal frame of reference of the child or student and supporting responsible action as it emerges from within. It means affording opportunities for action rather than assigning them. It means nurturing independent solving of problems rather than dictating the search for answers. Thus autonomy grows when there is, from parent and teacher, support for autonomy.

Finally, autonomy progresses only when the challenges to its exercise are themselves optimal. Challenges that are too great and result in pervasive failure only lower confidence and willingness to try. The exercise of autonomous capacities can proceed only from what one can already do. Under conditions of optimal challenge, those current capacities can be strengthened and elaborated. Finally, challenges which are too easy simply will not be engaged without outside prompt or reward. They are, in fact, experienced as boring and thus will be engaged only for extrinsic reasons. In sum, to facilitate autonomy, conditions for its exercise must be tailored to the developmental level and skill from which the individual starts.

The reasoning employed here then suggests a set of propositions capable of empirical exploration. They include the following:

1 Autonomy is essential to self-motivation. When autonomy is experienced, motivation, interest and desire for challenge are associated characteristics.

2 Children develop autonomy, self-motivation, and self-regulation to a greater degree under conditions where adults support autonomy.

3 Emphasis on controlling behaviour and salient use of external pressures and rewards undermines the sense of autonomy, and leads to lower self-regulatory capacities.

4 Autonomy is essential to self-esteem. Self-esteem develops, that is, only when one's own actions and interactions are valued and supported.

5 The development of autonomy is a transactional process. The more it is supported the more it obtains. However, the less it is in evidence the less likely adults are to support autonomy and the more likely they are instead to control or enforce compliance.

6 Autonomy will tend to be exercised under conditions of optimal challenge. Challenges too great or too easy are inimical to its expression.

These and other related propositions are what are explored in the research detailed herein.

So far, we have suggested that the movement toward autonomy is a natural developmental process. We have stated that it is important to capitalize on children's innate tendencies in this direction by providing educational experiences congruent with them, i.e., circumstances in which learning is experienced as autonomously motivated and in which feelings of effectance can take root. In our first proposition, the empirical evidence for which we will explore in this section, we suggested that whether or not children experience support for their autonomy in the classroom can have important concomitants, not only for children's achievement and learning per se, but also for their emotional adjustment and motivation. Schools, because they are such a pervasive socializing influence, shape many aspects of development including children's self-esteem, perceptions of control, and values. Viewed in this way, experience of autonomy can have far-reaching consequences.

Deci, Nezlek and Sheinman explored children's experiences of support for autonomy versus of being controlled within the classroom. They used a measure developed by DeCharms to assess the extent to which children experience their teachers' behaviour and the classroom climate as supportive of autonomy or as controlling. The experience of an autonomy-supportive climate involved children's seeing themselves as initiating their learning behaviour and as active participants in the classroom. Experiencing the classroom as controlling, on the other hand, involved experiencing the teacher as directing their learning behaviour, and themselves as more passive. Deci *et al.*, administered this questionnaire to 610 children from 35 classrooms. They also had children complete a survey developed by Harter which assessed children's motivation in the classroom. This scale measures three motivational tendencies: preference for challenge, curiosity, and independent mastery attempts, which are combined to provide an index of children's mastery motivation. Children's descriptions of their classrooms on the autonomy-support to control dimension were then correlated with children's mastery motivation, perceived competence in school, and self-esteem. The results of this study indicated significant relations between children's experiences of the classroom and intrinsic motivation. Children experiencing the classroom as more autonomy supportive described themselves as more intrinsically motivated for school than those experiencing the classroom environment as more controlling. Further, there were relations between perceptions of the environment and both perceived competence and self-esteem. Children describing the classroom as more supportive of their autonomy viewed themselves as more competent in school and had higher self-esteem than those seeing the classroom as more controlling.

In a related study, we attempted both to replicate these important findings as well as expand upon them by investigating possible source of children's perceptions of the classroom environment as either supportive of or controlling autonomy. In this study, we administered DeCharms' origin-climate questionnaire. We found that children's experiences of themselves in the classroom on this autonomy-support dimension had important consequences not only for their intrinsic motivation but for other self-related cognitions and affects. These results suggested that the more autonomy supportive the children perceived their classroom environments to be, the more mastery motivation they reported for school. Furthermore, children describing their classrooms as higher on the autonomy-support dimension described themselves as more competent in school and had higher self-esteem more generally than those seeing the classroom as more controlling. Thus, this study replicated that of Deci, Nezlek and Sheinman. In addition, the more autonomy supportive in nature the children perceived their classroom to be, the more they perceived school success and failure to be internally controlled and the less they saw control of outcomes in school in the hands of powerful others such as the teacher or reported that they did not know who or what controlled success and failure outcomes in school.

In a second phase of the study these children were asked to write a projective story about an ambiguous classroom scene. Those who had previously reported a more controlling atmosphere depicted more passive students and more authoritarian teachers in their stories than children who saw their classroom as more autonomy supportive. Thus, the perceived classroom environment has ramifications for how children organize and interpret their environment more generally.

The Ryan and Grolnick study thus demonstrated that there is great variability in the extent to which children experience themselves as autonomous in the classroom and that children's perceptions of themselves on this dimension have important consequences for motivation and affects with regard to both school and the self. If facilitating experiences of autonomy in the classroom is a goal for education, it would be important to understand the sources of these individual differences. How is it that some children feel more autonomous in school than others? In the same study, we explored two sources of variance in the way in which children experience their classrooms: differences *between* classrooms and individual differences between children *within* classrooms. Between-classroom differences were described by the average classroom climate score for al children in a given classroom while within-classroom differences referred to within-classroom variation from the particular classroom mean. We found, first, that there were average differences between classrooms in experienced autonomy. Such between-classroom differences suggest that teachers provide certain contexts for learning which facilitate differing experiences of autonomy for the children in their classrooms. These results, then, point to the importance of the climate provided by the teacher for children's experiences of autonomy or lack thereof.

However, the results also showed that even within classrooms there was great variability in the extent to which self-determination or autonomy was experienced. In fact, the individual difference component or experiences in the classroom largely accounted for relations between the classroom climate measure and self-related variables. This finding suggests that, irrespective of the teacher, there are aspects of the children which lead them to experience themselves as more or less autonomous. One possibility for understanding these individual differences in perceived autonomy is that children may behave in such a way that they are actually treated differentially by the teacher and so feel more or less self-determined in the classroom. A second possibility is that children come into the classroom with tendencies toward experiencing themselves as more or less autonomous and these tendencies affect how they experience the teacher and classroom. One possible explanation for the latter account is that experiences of home environments may shape tendencies to see other environments and caretakers in particular ways. Thus, some of the experience of autonomy in the classroom appears to be derived from classroom experiences while another part is derived from children's characteristics and possibly their histories with caretakers. In the next sections of the chapter, we will explore the importance of teachers and parents in facilitating autonomy in children.

The role of the classroom environment

The Ryan and Grolnick study revealed that there are differences between classrooms in the extent to which children experience themselves as self-determining or autonomous. These findings suggest that teachers may have an important role in facilitating such classroom experiences. There have been a number of studies focusing on one particular aspect of teachers: the extent to which they are supportive or controlling of children's autonomy. Deci, Nezlek and Sheinman suggested that teachers have characteristic tendencies toward dealing with children that can be viewed as ranging from supporting children's autonomy to controlling children's behaviour. These authors reasoned that some teachers believe that children should be controlled and that they know what is best for the children. These teachers tend to use controls such as rewards, evaluations or grades, and threats to get children to learn and to solve problems that come up in the classroom. These techniques lead children to experience their behaviour and learning in school as instrumental to achieve such rewards or grades rather than as self-determined. Other teachers believe that it is important for children to be able to solve their own problems and see their role to facilitate such independent thought and decision making. They tend to try to involve children in the process of learning by giving them choices. These teachers tend to support children's problem-solving attempts by using discussion and other autonomy-promoting techniques rather than by imposing their own solutions onto the children.

Before examining the effects of teachers' orientations on the autonomy-support to control dimension, it is important to clarify that an autonomy-supportive context for learning is not a permissive one. The autonomy-supportive classroom is not one where there is complete freedom for children to do whatever they want. Rather, there is a good deal of consistent structure imposed by teachers. The determining factor in autonomy-supportive versus controlling classrooms is, then, not whether there are rules, disciplinary techniques and directives, but, rather, the way in which these structures are imposed and extent to which choices and independence are encouraged when possible. The issue of imposing limits in an autonomy-supportive context will be discussed at larger strength later in this section.

Deci, Schwartz, Sheinman and Ryan developed a measure of teachers' orientations on the autonomy-support to control dimension. Teachers' orientations, as measured by this scale, were then correlated with the mastery motivation and self-evaluations of the children in their classrooms. The results of these analyses revealed significant relations between teacher orientations and these variables such that the more autonomy-supportive the teacher, the higher the mastery motivation children reported and the higher their perceived competence in school and in general. Although these findings suggest that teachers' orientations on the autonomy-support to control continuum can have important consequences for the motivation and self-related affects of children, the corr:lational nature of this study leaves the direction of influence undermined. One explanation for these findings is that motivational orientations of the children in the classrooms leads teaches to take on more autonomy oriented or more controlling styles.

In order to further understand the meaning of these correlational results, Deci *et al.* measured children's mastery motivation, perceived competence and self-esteem on day two of the school year and again eight weeks later. They reasoned that any change in these children variables occurring between the first days of school and later in the year could be accounted for by the teacher and classroom environment. The results indicated that teachers' orientations toward support versus control of children's autonomy were predictive of change on these children variables such that more controlling the teacher, the greater tl, decrements in mastery motivation, perceived cognitive competence and self-esteem across the eight week interval.

The results of the above studies point to the importance of teachers' styles in facilitating children's desire to take on challenging material and their curiosity in school. Another issue, probably even more crucial for development and for adjustment in the classroom, because much of what is taught in school is not inherently interesting, concerns children's attitudes or orientations toward school and the learning process. Ryan, Connell and Deci have reasoned that children take on different orientations toward engaging in school-related activities which are not inherently interesting or fun. Some children will engage in such activities only because of external contingencies or pressures imposed by caretakers, i.e., because they will either get in trouble if they don't comply or because of imposed directives. These children tend to be externally oriented in their learning behaviour. On the other hand, some children have taken upon themselves the motivation and responsibility for their own learning. They may not always like the activities they do in school and learning and so have internalized the regulation of their school activity. These different orientations toward regulating school behaviour can be placed along a continuum according to how self-determined children are for their school behaviour. Connell and Ryan have developed a questionnaire called the Self-Regulation Questionnaire to assess children's characteristic styles of self-regulation on this self-determination continuum. The questionnaire yields a summary score called the Self-Determination Index which describes children's placement along the self-determination continuum.

In recent study, Grolnick and Ryan explored the relation of teachers' orientations toward support versus control of autonomy to children's self-regulation on the self-determination continuum. In order to do this, they performed a short-term longitudinal analysis of changes in children's self-determination for learning across the first five months of the school year. Elementary school children in grades 3-6 from 20 classrooms completed the Self-Regulation Questionnaire on day two of the school year and again in February of the same year. Teachers completed the Problems in School Questionnaire early in the school year. It was found that children who were in the classrooms of more autonomy-supportive teachers increased in their identification with the value and importance of achievement-related behaviours between the two assessments relative to children of more controlling teachers. Thus, even when activities or information taught in the classroom are not intrinsically or inherently motivating, teachers' styles can be important in helping children to move towards self-determination or autonomy for their learning.

As stated earlier, supporting autonomy, especially when activities or materials to be learned are not inherently motivating, does not mean allowing children to do whatever they want. Teachers often need to set limits or rules about what needs to be accomplished in the classroom. Supporting autonomy is not antithetical to limits; rather, it implies a particular manner in which limits are conveyed, i.e., one in which limits are stated matter-of-factly without language making salient pressure and control and in which children's feelings about the limits are acknowledged. Same limits could be communicated in a controlling or noncontrolling manner and that, whereas the former would be likely to undermine intrinsic motivation, the latter would maintain or enhance it.

In their study, Koestner *et al.* set limits on first and second grade children's neatness in a painting activity. In the controlling group, children were told that they should keep the materials and themselves neat so they would have to wear a smock, keep the paints neat and not spill them. The noncontrolling group was given the same limits and directions with two subtle differences. First, the words 'should' and 'have to' were not used. Secondly, it was acknowledged that they may not feel like doing these things but they were being asked to do them nonetheless. For example, the experimenter said, 'I know that sometimes it's fun to slop paint around, but for now, please keep it on the small center sheet.' By acknowledging the potential conflict for the child, it is reasoned that a power struggle between adult and child can be avoided and the child can accept the limit without a loss of self-esteem. These principles are central to Ginottian limit setting.

The results of the study revealed that children who had been given controlling limits were subsequently less intrinsically motivated to paint relative to those receiving noncontrolling who did not differ from a no-limit comparison group. Children did not however differ in the degree of compliance. This study demonstrated that it is possible to limit children's behaviour without understanding their sense of autonomy and so their motivation. This illustrates that autonomy support can include firmness and structure along with a willingness to support choice and independence.

The role of parents

The previously discussed studies suggest that teacher styles can have important consequences for children's motivation and self-determination in the classroom. By allowing them autonomy and supporting their independent efforts to solve their own problems they help children to move toward taking more responsibility for their school-related behaviour and so require less external control and pressure. However, as stated earlier, children enter the classroom with widely different motivational orientations on the self-determination continuum. These may be in part a function of previous classroom experiences. It seems plausible, however, that at least part of their attitudes and orientations may be a function of the orientations of another major socializing influence, namely parents.

In a recently completed series of studies, we hypothesized that parents who tend to control children's autonomy at home should interfere with their children's movement toward self-regulation was expected to be manifest not only in children's descriptions of themselves as less self-determining on the Self-Regulation Questionnaire, but also in higher levels of adjustment difficulties in the classroom as rated by their teachers. Failures of self-regulation are evident to the extent that children do not behave appropriately or follow classroom procedures. In addition, children's tendencies to stay focused on tasks which they are expected to work on and to have good study and work habits are also a reflection of their ability to be self-regulating with regard to their school behaviour. We thus included teacher ratings of children's acting-out and learning problems in the classroom. It was also expected that parental orientations on the autonomy-support to control continuum would be related to children's self-evaluations. Our reasoning was that it is only when one feels a sense of ownership or self-determination for behaviour that positive experiences and feedback will affect self-evaluation.

In one attempt to explore these possible parental contributions to children's autonomy in school, Ryan, Deci and Grolnick developed a survey to assess children's perceptions of their mothers and fathers on the autonomy-support to control continuum. This measure, called the Parent Orientation Scale, was administered to children from three different school districts. Approximately 450 rural, 560 suburban, and 450 urban children completed the Parent Orientation Scale as well as other questionnaires rapping their self-evaluations and motivation in school. In addition, teachers rated children on rating scales tapping competence and motivation in the classroom. Children's perceptions of their parents on the autonomy-support dimension were then examined for relations with these children related variables.

The results of this study suggested that parental autonomy support, as experienced by the child, had a number of significant school-related concomitants. Specifically, children who saw their parents as more school and in general than those describing their parents as more controlling. Furthermore, perceptions of autonomy-supportive parents, especially mothers, were associated with higher levels of mastery motivation and more self-determined motivational orientations in children. Perceptions of autonomy support were also positively associated with higher teacher ratings of competence and ability in children. Relations between children's perceptions of their parents and teacher ratings were particularly strong for girls.

Thus the above results point to the importance of perceived parental autonomy support for children's self-determination and competence in school. Also in the Ryan, Deci and Grolnick study, the relations between children's perceptions of their parents' autonomy support and their perceptions of the teacher and classroom environment were examined It was reasoned that children who experiences their parents as more controlling might tend to see their classroom environment as more controlling than those who see their home environment as supporting their autonomy. Correlational analyses confirmed this hypothesis. Thus, the perceived parental environment may set the stage not only for self-related cognitions and affects with regard to school but also the way in which the teacher is experienced. The lack of a feeling of self-determination or autonomy may then create a self-fulfilling prophecy where the child expects control and acts in such a way that the teacher must respond controllingly to get the child to do his or her work.

As was the case with studies exploring children's perceptions of the classroom environment, the fact that the environment was viewed through the child's eyes makes it impossible to confirm the hypothesis that actual parent orientations affect children's self-determination in the classroom. A more direct assessment of parental styles was thus a focus of another study conducted by Grolick and Ryan.

Grolnick and Ryan interviewed mothers and fathers of 48 third through sixth grade children from a rural elementary school. The focus of this interview was on the ways in which the parent motivates his or her child to engage in school and home-related activities such as doing homework as well as the way the parent responds when his or her child exhibits positive or negative behaviour with respect to the particular activity. Parents' responses to the series of interview questions were rated by two independent raters on three component scales associated with the autonomy-support to control dimension. The three component scales measured the following aspects of autonomy support: *value autonomy* was the extent to which the parent valued the child's autonomy and saw its promotion as a goal versus valued obedience and conformity first and foremost. *Autonomy-promoting techniques* reflected the extent to which the parent employed autonomy-oriented motivational and disciplinary techniques such as reasoning, encouragement and emphathic limit setting versus relying on controlling, power assertive methods such as physical punishment or controlling rewards. And *non-directiveness* was defined as the extent to which the parent includes the child in decisions and problem solving versus imposes his or here own agenda on the child. A parent's score for autonomy support was the average of his or here ratings on the three scales. Maternal, paternal, and combined parent ratings were then related to children's self-determination, behavioural adjustment, and perceived competence with respect to school.

The results of this interview study provided support for the hypothesized relations between parental autonomy support and children's autonomy in the classroom. Children whose parents were rated as more supportive of autonomy were more self-determined in the classroom than those who parents were rated as more controlling. In addition, children of more autonomy-supportive parents were rated by their teachers as displaying less acting-out problems in the classroom and as having fewer learning difficulties than those of more controlling parents, suggesting that children of autonomy-supportive parents are more likely to internalize the rules and regulations of their classrooms. Parental autonomy support was also positively associated with various indices of children's school-related competence, including achievement scores, grades, and teacher-rated competence. In these relations, maternal autonomy support was generally more strongly related than paternal autonomy support. However, the strongest relations were usually for the overall parental environment. There was also a marginally significant positive relation between maternal autonomy support and children's perceived competence in the academic domain.

The above findings suggest that, through their support for autonomy and independence in their children, parents prepare their children for a school environment requiring self-regulation and autonomous functioning. More controlling parental styles may have the effect of forestalling the developmental movement toward autonomy and self-regulation in children making it necessary for teachers to motivate these children through prodding and pushing. It is easy to see how such a pernicious cycles of control is perpetuated.

Autonomy in children's learning — Quality and quantity

In these studies we have reviewed so far, we have shown that autonomy in the classroom has important consequences for children's self-related cognitions and motivational orientation in school. We have also provided some evidence that children's positions along the developmental continuum of autonomy may be at least in part a function of the degree of autonomy support provided by significant others such as parents and teachers. Thus, facilitating self-determination in the classroom may be presumed to be an important goal for teachers. It might be argued, however, that the bottom line for educational goals must be learning outcomes *per se*. From this viewpoint, the prime argument for increased autonomy in the classroom would come from evidence that it facilitates actual learning and retention of information. Addressing this issue, we suggest that children's autonomy in the learning process may, in fact, have important consequences for learning outcomes, particularly with regard to the quality of learning.

The issue of 'quality' is learning is a complex one. Most of the practical assessment tools used to measure learning outcomes in educational contexts emphasize quantitative rather than qualitative dimensions, and thus ignore important aspects of what skilled facilitation of learning can impart. For our part we would define the qualitative aspects of learning not in terms of the accretion of rote facts, but rather in terms of the integration of what is learned into a long-term knowledge base; and the ability and willingness to transfer and apply that knowledge in new situations. These qualitative aspects, in other words, are reflections of the *integration* of what is learned.

The integration of learning we believe to be an active process requiring self-determination on the part of the learner. Benware and Deci recently made this point in a study examining learning under an active versus passive motivational set. When college students learned material expecting to teach it to another student, their conceptual understanding of the material was enhanced relative to that of students learning the material because they expected a graded test would follow.

Grolnick and Ryan recently conducted a study examining both varied learning contexts and individual differences in motivational styles in children as they related to the quantity of learning in a reading comprehension task. In this study, fifth grade children were asked to read a grade level passage from a social studies book under one of three learning conditions: controlling-directed, non-controlling-directed, and non-directed. These conditions varied in the extent to which autonomy for learning was afforded. In the controlling-directed condition, children were told to read the material because they would be tested and graded for their learning. In this condition, evaluation and pressure were salient thus creating a situation where children felt externally controlled. In the non-controlling-directed (NCD) condition, children were asked to read the same passage and were told that they should be asked questions about it later. The focus, however, was on learning the material for its own sake. Evaluation and pressure were nonsalient thus creating a context where children might feel relatively more autonomous. In a third condition, the nondirected (ND) condition, children were asked to read the grade level material but were not told that they would be tested or asked questions later. It was presumed that, since there was no explicit direction to learn the material, any learning that did take place would be the result of the children's own internal proneness or tendency. Thus, the ND condition involved the highest relative degree of autonomy.

6

Curriculum Integration and Development

Special education, the education of exceptional children and youth, has grown rapidly during the past two decades, both in numbers served and resources expended. such strides have not been without significant growing pains. In responding to the plight of exceptional students floundering in or excluded from regular classrooms, educators created a specialized service delivery system and a set of curricula that were both more supportive and more restrictive. Now, after a decade since the passage of Public Law 94-142, newly gained knowledge, experience, values, and resources have returned the focus to the merging of general and special education, and an important question persists: How should the curriculum for these students be planned? As an integral part of the curriculum for all students or different from the curriculum for those considered as "normal" nonhandicapped students?

This chapter presents a position for exploring several dimensions of the major questions and a set of alternative solutions for solving the problem. The remainder of the chapter provides arguments to illustrate contrasting views and emphasis in measuring student progress through the curriculum.

Defining the curriculum and its relationship to instruction

The Curriculum myth

Should the curriculum for exceptional or handicapped students be the same as or different from the curriculum for nonhandicapped students?

Before answering such a question, one should first pause to ask at least the following questions:

How does one define "curriculum"?

Are "same as" and "different from" the only two choices or are they points along a continuum of responses?

In instruction a concept related to or apart from the definition of curriculum?

Can we really talk about "handicapped students" and "nonhandicapped students" as two sets of individuals distinctly different from one another?

Further development of these major questions should point to implications for addressing the development of the curriculum in regular and special education.

A seemingly obvious but necessary consideration may be whether or not a curriculum exists for nonhandicapped students at the local school district level. In many districts across the country, there is something of a "curriculum myth," that is, that a unified, coordinated course of study, complete with a philosophy, goals, and an evaluation scheme exists. The myth further suggests that there is an articulation between grade levels and that all key stakeholders understand its implementation. More typically, the curriculum is a set of courses based on standards that closely reflect the graduation requirements of the state agency. An inquirer may, in some instances, collect differing responses depending on whether the respondent is a central office administrator or a fifth grade teacher. In short, there is ambiguity and confusion in terms.

Curriculum and instruction

Curriculum is often viewed as a part of instruction, teaching, and learning, not as a distinctive concept independent of the other three. MacDonald explains, "at the present it is well to recognize that there is no consistently clear distinction in use of much educational terminology." He offers a set of definitions. The curriculum system consists of persons who are a part of a social system that evolves in a curriculum, that is, a plan of action. MacDonald agrees that the boundary between curriculum and instruction is the key. He says, "they are essentially two separate action contexts, one producing plans for further action; and the other putting plans into action." Using a system perspective, he suggests that the "professionally oriented behaviour of individual personality systems, called teachers by society, makes up the acts of teaching." Learning is the "phenomena or behaviour that is noted in the performance of the student." Teaching and learning make up the components of the instructional system. The instructional system is a social system, not a personality system. It is the action context within which formal teaching and learning behaviours take place.

Since each system is bounded, it excludes the possibility of any of the four areas being included in any other space. MacDonald observes, "traditionally, the tendency has been to include instruction within curriculum, and teaching and learning within the instructional setting. This position is impossible to defend from a systems position." Then, "teaching is defined as the behaviour of the teacher, learning as the change in learner behaviour, instruction as the pupil-teacher interaction situation and curriculum as those planning endeavours which take place prior to instruction."

An important distinction needs to be made between the terms "curriculum" and "instruction." If we view the curriculum *per se* as the broader course of study, the expectations and values that a district holds for all students, and instruction as the act or practice of teaching students to become independent, then we could generalize that the same expectations hold for the handicapped learner. Even of the severely and profoundly disabled, in spite of their dependency, the curriculum ought to be more "same" and the instruction is the variable that may be more "different."

The role of values in curriculum development

Cultural determinism

Before moving to a discussion of sameness versus difference in curriculum development and the distinction between types of handicapped or exceptional students, a short description of the primary values that drive curriculum development is in order.

A primary purpose of education has been the transmission of knowledge across generations, transforming a human organism with potential for learning into a social being. This is accomplished as the customary ways of behaving, speaking, and thinking that have accumulated over time in various cultures are acquired and put into practice by the individual. Enculturation establishes the basis for coordinated group activity and is essential for group survival.

It is rare, however, even in technologically simple, small-scale societies, for an individual to learn all there is to know of his or her culture. This is true both because any cultural repertoire is large whereas the individual's capacity to cope with information is limited and selective and because certain individuals are systematically excluded from access to different kinds of knowledge on the basis of their status. Key questions to be asked of the educational process in any society include the following:

What kinds of knowledge and behaviour are shared by virtually all members of a society and are considered *essential* for membership?

What kinds of knowledge and behaviour are shared by some but not all members of the society and therefore constitute *cultural alternatives*?

What are the criteria for determining what is *appropriate* for individuals within a society and who should learn certain types of knowledge and behaviour?

In the United States the major part of each individual's knowledge and behaviour falls in the category of "cultural alternatives." Biological and social factors have typically affected what alternatives are presented to whom and under what circumstances. The handicapped, as a class, have joined other historically suspect legal classifications into which students are groups for learning, such as age, sex, race, measured ability, religious affiliation, and class status.

in classifying students as handicapped, questionable practices of assessment have had a profound impact on the labeling of individuals as retarded, emotionally disturbed, and so on for their education, however appropriately or inappropriately. Classically, education for the retarded, therefore, has historical roots in being "different" with such development by Itard, Sequin, and Montessori. According to Goldstein, the curriculum for the learning disabled was more often the "same" and without any kind of necessary modification.

Minimally handicapped students, on the other hand, whose special learning problems were less apparent and not assessed were often found "in the back rows" of regular classrooms and/or were retained from year to year until they voluntarily dropped out. They experienced their education, never identified as being handicapped, with consequently fewer educational alternatives than they might have deserved. The more severely and profoundly handicapped students have either never been in school or were directed into special classes, separate facilities, or institutions outside of the public school system. As a result, they have often been denied access to educational alternatives and basic enculturating experiences provided for their nonhandicapped peers.

Much rethinking about exceptional student education was a necessary result of litigation and research around the following:

1. Lack of clear evidence showing superior educational achievement among handicapped students taught in special classes and institutions in comparison with those taught in a regular setting

2. Evidence of the harmful social effects of segregation on both sets of students in and out of the "mainstream"
3. Abuses of the special education system in that special programs became "dumping grounds" for behaviour problem students and minorities as federal funding for the effort increased
4. Inappropriate discriminatory labeling and testing of children referred and placed in special education programs and the disproportionate numbers of minorities being placed in such classes, resulting in stereotypical behaviours and consequences difficult to "correct"
5. Questionable preconceptions about the abilities, disabilities, and learning styles of the learning disabled and the mentally handicapped in terms of learning potential versus limitations
6. Increased pressure on state and local school districts to be educationally and fiscally responsible for their handicapped population regardless of the handicapping condition or the burden of cost
7. Equal educational opportunity in terms of civil, access to programs and facilities, and so on.

Martin argued that P.L. 94-142, affirmed the rights of the handicapped to a free, appropriate, public education in the least restrictive environment and mandated that IEPs for all handicapped students would ensure such rights. With this act, handicapped and nonhandicapped learners would be considered more alike than different and should be so treated in public school.

Klein, Pasch, and Frew believe that special education leadership personnel had an opportunity early to seize the initiative to bring the best from regular and special education together to improve the learning experiences for all children. To date, despite these aspirations, some attempts and few successes can be reported.

A continuum of contrasting cultural values

Underlying the points of view expressed over time on both the educational status of the handicapped and on what is an appropriate curriculum for handicapped learners are sets of values that might be found along a continuum of pluralistic values as "conservative/pragmatic" on one end and "experimental/egalitarian" on the other.

Some examples of views representing such a values conflict that affect decisions regarding our major curriculum questions are the following:

Conservative/Pragmatic	*Experimental/Egalitarian*
Learning capabilities or aptitudes of individuals are largely beyond the capacity of education to change.	Learning capabilities or aptitudes are malleable, dynamic and can be significantly changed by education.
Individuals within a society are better able to serve in appropriate roles when tested, labeled, and grouped homogeneously in cost-effective educational and occupational training.	All students must have access to as full a range of educational opportunities as possible for as long as possible because judgments of aptitude are premature when used early to determine long-range placements means of measuring aptitude are biased and inadequate categories underlying such placements have been poorly devised advances in instructional technology may unlock learner potential previously unsuspected.

Human and fiscal resources should be concentrated in improved education for non-dependent persons such that they are then better able to contribute to the improvement of life and society as a whole. This is more cost-effective in that gains are more measurable.	Resources invested in improved education of dependent persons will likely reduce their dependency for a lifetime. Personal and economic benefits accrue for all members of a society in the long run by increasing the number of contributing members and reducing the life-long economic burden of such alternatives as institutionalization.
Individual's responsibilities are to serve and to adapt to society as a whole.	Society's institutions must adjust to facilitate the full educational development of the individual. A society so reformed will benefit from a vastly increased reservoir of human resources.

There are some obvious ramifications for educating students from this values conflict. While holding high expectations for all students, one must certainly allow for vast individual differences.

Three colleagues at Syracuse University published a debate over educating mentally retarded students. Winschel, Ensher, and Blatt argue for an emphasis on different sides of the continuum. Winschel, who proposes that the emphasis in the curriculum should be on "learning to learn," states that educators ought to be advocates for the eradication of retardation. He identifies four cognitive skills that handicapped learners must develop: listening, remembering, reflective behaviour, and problem solving. Strategies for developing these skills have been more evident in the research than in practice. Faith in the "malleability of intelligence" demands that these foundation skills be learned even at the expense of the mastery of normalizing skills. Ensher, who stresses a "learning to do" approach, argues that "growth in adaptive behaviour in order to achieve the least dependent position possible within school, home, and society" is clearly the purpose of education and that training insufficiently grounded in the practical may be a disservice to the moderately and severely handicapped.

"Learning to be" is the position Blatt advocates; he calls for an "infusion of creative thinking" into the field as well as a willingness to experiment with new and unorthodox methods and materials. For Blatt, both teaching an learning are parts of an ongoing process. "Always, the core is to be, to know who one is and thus to stand for something...the aim always being the comprehension of oneself in a larger context." A curriculum focus leading to increased self-confidence appears to be the primary contribution of Blatt's view.

Burrello, Tracy, and Schultz believe a key issue in this debate, as in the value conflict, is that the consequences of being handicapped are as much the result of a technological failure to transmit knowledge and skills as they are persistent limitations of the individual versus the view that deficits are innate and mostly unrelenting and that, pragmatically speaking, gains are too marginal and too costly to attain through publicly supported educational programs and/or services.

Frew comes close to providing a basis for a synthesis of these value systems in his attempt to bring together regular and special education through curriculum analysis and design. All learning is developmental. His Functional Life curriculum joins the learning of functional skills to the acquisition of such basic skills as reading, writing, and arithmetic in "the major areas of human activity—sociocultural, economic, political, and personal development."

> The old excuse that we are unsure of the overall potential for achievement will no longer work. The time has come to determine what to teach systematically and to continue instructional sequences as long as the student is learning and applying them appropriately.

The kind of thinking exemplified in his Functional Life Curriculum, together with the movement toward an individualized educational program, suggest that the old distinctions among "academic," "career," "vocational," and "remedial" may be breaking down. By analogy with our perception of children's learning styles, we may come to see these types of curricula as occupying a continuum. They shade into and penetrate one another. Such a view would imply major changes in the way teachers are trained, in the way specialty areas are carved out, and in the way curriculum decisions are made from the top administrative level to the classroom.

If the education of the exceptional student will contribute anything of both immediate and lasting value to education in general, it is the process dimension of curricular decisionmaking, the individual education program planning process. By imposing such a structure, the IEP process allows educators to identify the needs of handicapped students and systematically formulate methods and stipulate resources needed for meeting those needs. It is a tool by which the "whole child" can be reviewed. If all children were able to benefit from such a process, a "whole curriculum" would need to be created as well. In this way, a curriculum could be designed to occupy a continuum with no absolute beginnings or endings and much room for expansion in many directions.

Development of strategies for an integrated curriculum

While it is impossible to project all the circumstances around curriculum development or reform movements, we have attempted to describe responses to two general sets of conditions. The first if one where the special education leadership is attempting to build linkages into an already existing curriculum; the second is one where a curriculum reform movement is underway.

7

Current Educational Theory

Humanist educational theory

What we have not done yet is to investigate from a narrower perspective whether there is not a self-described. A suitable way to answer this question would seem to offer itself immediately through the other history of the term humanist than the one that has occupied out attention so far. From this alternative perspective it actually comes to describe both a kind of learning and the kind of scholarship related to this learning. The 'humanist' as a scholar was one dedicated to 'learning for learning's sake, otium, remaining within the limits of human knowledge, aimed at neither transcendence not particle purposes. The 15th century 'humanista' in the Italian universities studied and taught humanae litterae. These usages of the term in its different derivations within the other European languages have remained constant since through the centuries that have' followed, not withstanding some temporary aberrations. One would therefore be traditional humanistic curriculum must constitute the central focus of any current self-defined humanist education programme if any exist. It therefore comes as some surprise to read the following comment:

> Humanistic education is more a diffuse and multiplex phenomenon than one that may be sharply caught and defined. Although in its own apologies it distinguishes itself quite dramatically from other educational systems, its rationale is elusive and the educationist must find his way through a series of exhortations, general statements on education and life, anecdotes of personal success, and recipes for particular methods. One rarely finds extended statements of educational theory that give enough detail and elaborated justification with which to concur or not.

For it is immediately clear that the article from which it is taken cannot be referring to the same tradition.

In point of fact Williams and Foster, the joint authors of the article, while making this evaluation, cite as their point of reference an entry that appeared in the 1971-72 Education Index, where mention is made of a 'new' humanism in current educational thought. Not only does this 'new' humanism show no continuity with this tradition, it also shows no continuity whatsoever with that faith in the power of human institutions to contribute towards the betterment of life which Baier identified as part of the modern conception of humanism inherited from the Renaissance. On the contrary it is extremely sceptical, if not downright antagonistic, towards all forms of institutionalized learning, most especially schooling, and emphasises the value of personal autonomy in its most radical form. In fact, for the roots of the kind of theoretical individualism suggested by the 'new' humanism one needs to go back to the anti-Enlightenment naturalistic philosophy of Rousseau's Emile, which similarly aligns itself 'in favour of the individual as an educational good in itself, and as prior to consideration of the individual's contribution to society'.

Power, independently of Williams and Foster, writes about 'romantic' humanism as constituting a distinctive if ill-defined trend in contemporary educational theory. He also attributes to this trend the same characteristics attributed to the 'new' humanism by the latter, distinguishing within it the same kind of radical subjectivism and eventually describing its as follows:

> What we shall call romantic humanism exudes an abundance of self-sufficiency and self-confidence. Tilting on the verge of arrogance it turns its back on the past, finds nothing of much worth in tradition, and justifies the motives of each person to find his own satisfaction in a face-to-fact confrontation with reality.

It is interesting to note that the basis of the 'arrogance' identified by Power arises not from a faith in science but in a faith in the self-sufficiency of the individual. It denotes a courage which was impossible for the philosopher of the polis, who was firmly convinced that the very nature of human being is social, and is unacceptable for philosophers who present a communal ideal of man, like Marx and Dewey. It was forced, briefly, on the 'skeptical' philosophers of the Hellenistic schools, nearly conclusively buried by Christian theology, and finally revived in a most resounding manner by Nietzsche's pronouncement that 'God is dead'; his metaphor not only for the dissolution of religious faith but for 'the devaluation of our hitherto highest values'—those of the Enlightenment as much as any other. Nietzsche's pronouncement, of course, later became the point of departure of atheistic existentialism.

Existentialists have consistently rejected the notion that their analysis of the human condition properly constitutes a 'philosophy' in the usual sense of the word where it applies to the systematization of thought into the disciplined formal expression of theories. Their position is that no such systematization is possible, nor is it required, to this extent they even reject the necessity of science. They argue that the generalizations to which systematization leads are necessarily false, and this is a view that is tacitly echoed by the 'new' or 'romantic' humanists. Both Williams and Foster, and Power, in fact, on serve the discomfort of 'romantic' humanists with philosophy, and Power confirms that their orientation instead towards the kind of psychology connected with the personality theories of Rogers and Maslow, is pursued at the expense of philosophy which 'scarcely gets a look-in'. The general situation in this respect is that.

> Few humanists are eager to shape any systematic philosophy of education, and many of them worry about the stultifying effect such systematization could have on education aspirations.

For this reason one cannot properly speak of 'romantic' humanism as constituting a 'school', though the word movement may not be inapt since it allows for a greater degree of permissiveness in the ranks, though even a movement needs some coordinating ideas and principles in order to be so defined beyond the rejection of a systematic philosophy of education. The radical writers identified with it by the authors represent, in fact, a group brought together not by any unified perspective on educational practice but by their general dissatisfaction with 'school' ad other manifestations of institutionalized learning, a dissatisfaction that, at times, borders on nihilism. So the resemblances are clearly there, and it comes as no surprise when Poser suggests that if one were to 'shop around' for a philosophical position with which 'romantic' humanism could align itself, the natural choice would be existentialism, for, as he says, it alone has the temperament that would appeal to the new humanism's 'romantic' orientations. At the same time, however, we are also warned by Power not to make too much of this fact of this fact because, he says, though 'romantic' humanists may eventually claim existentialism as their creed, this is not the case at the moment, nor is any such alignment imminent judging by the actual state of the movement.

Existentialism

Richmond similarly says about lifelong education that 'Philosophically, it might be designated as an existentialist or phenomenological view'. At the same time a comment reminiscent of Power's about 'romantic' humanist education warns immediately that 'it seems advisable to refrain from any such pretentious labelling. It will also be recalled that when Cropley described humanism as the 'philosophy' of the lifelong education programmed he put the word 'philosophy' inside inverted commas, and said that the programme in fact could only 'loosely' be called humanistic. Again, it needs to be noted that when Richmond attaches the lifelong education programme philosophically with existentialism he does so without making any further qualifications; it must therefore be assumed that he is alluding not to some tendency within the movement but to the movements as a whole.

But it is clear that, on this last point, he cannot be right. This is because we have already uncovered different traits within the literature of the movement that have nothing to do with existentialism. And yet Richmond's observation is not wrong; it simply focuses on the literature from a different perspective to Cropley's and Ireland's. One recalls, for instance, in Cropley's own definition of lifelong education according to the UIE literature, that he refers to the ultimate aim of the programme as 'the self-fulfillment of each individual. The question was raised in that place as to how self-fulfillment could be conceived, in particular whether it can make space for the community, as Dave's lifelong education programme demands. If self-fulfillment is conceptualized subjectively, then it will be the basis for a different lifelong education programme wit orientations towards existentialism. Still, nowhere does one encounter any explicit statement of lifelong education as an existentialist programme. So Richamong can only be reading it into the movement's literature, just as it is only to be read into the 'romantic' humanist educational theory. Or elase the literature itself could be aligned with 'romantic' humanist theory directly perhaps?!

Before any incursions are made into this possibility, however, it is first necessary to say a little bit more about the relevant aspects of existentialism as a philosophy. It has already been observed that its pregenitors are taken to be Kierkegaard and Nietzsche. The first was primarily concerned with the question 'How can I become a Christian?' while the second asked the apparently contrary question how it is possible to live a Godless existence.

The point of similarity between the two lies in what they both denied, namely the standard or conventional solutions to the problems they posed, insisting instead on complete subjectivity—each and every individual must come upon truth and come to terms with it in his own way unaided by the pronouncements of popular opinion. For both the standard sought is that of authenticity. Kierkegaard's individual become authentic to the extent that his relationship with God is personalized, since although conformity with God's will is still the end of man, the content of that will cannot be known to humanity in the shape of universal principles. For Kierkegaard, in fact, the individual as a particular is higher than the universal and is justified against it not the other way around. While for Nietzsche authenticity lies in the pursuit of the ubermensche, of that 'higher self' which 'does not however lie deeply hidden within you, but immeasurably high above you, or, at least, above that which you usually take as yourself. For both, the authentic person is one who 'chooses himself', and authentic existence is one based on faith and commitment to it, rather than science and reason. This is how Passmore describes the convergence of their two philosophies into existentialism:

> Both philosophers concern themselves passionately, if diversely, with the human situation they both reject as a delusion all abstract, objective, systematic, philosophy for both of them 'life is more than logic'. It makes all the difference in the world, Nietzsche wrote, 'whether a thinker stands in personal relation to his problems, in which he sees his destiny, his need, and even his highest happiness, or can only feel and grasp them impersonally, with the

> tentacles of cold, prying thought'. That might be Kierkegaard talking - or any existentialist. Again, both Kierkegaard and Nietzsche see in 'essences' a device men use to tame the world, to reduce it to something indifferent and stable. The 'real' world, they tell us, is historical, 'existential', revealed as such to the courageous human agent, but lying beyond the understanding of abstract thought, which always, by its nature, deals in types. And Nietzsche, like Kierkegaard, bitterly attacks the Philistine, the mediocre man, whose highest ideal is to submerge himself - to do 'what is done', to be 'Man' as distinct from 'a man'.

The more representative figures in existentialist thought since have kept faith with this programme, emphasizing the subjective element in human life and relating it to the crucial questions of freedom, decision and responsibility as they converge on the problem of personal or authentic choice. Such choice is rendered difficult, according to the existentialist, by our 'facticity'; by the fact that we are thrown into a world that predates our existence and is not of our own making. We are, furthermore, made to struggle within it because of the very nature of our own Being which is different from that of other beings also thrown into the arena of life in the sense that we alone are self-conscious about our own existential predicament. Or, put in another way, human beings are the only beings whose existence is an issue for themselves, they are therefore the only beings whose relationship with the world is typically that of 'care'. This means that choice is always a necessary condition of human life, it is always, to some extent, inescapable, but it is only authentic choice that enables us to 'stand out' as individuals. Authentic choice, on the other hand, is the contrary of 'bad faith', and 'bad faith' consists as much in our failure to recognize our personal autonomy of choice as in our failure to recognize the significance of other moral consciousnesses in our lives besides our own.

Macquarrie, in fact, says that probably all the leading existentialists pay at least lip-service to the truth that man exists as a person only in a community of persons. But, at the same time, he continues to say: 'in the main they are concerned with the individual whose quest for authentic selfhood focuses on the meaning of personal being', to the extent in fact that they find themselves involved in paradox. This is because contrasting with their lip-service to the essential communality of human beings most existentialists retain a characteristic attitude to the 'Other' as one who, of necessity, by his very being, sabotages my possibility to make choice that are free. Within it the primordial relationship in which human beings stand to each other and to the rest of the community is one of conflict, as the 'Other' poses genuine limitations to the pursuit of personal authenticity. Furthermore, this latent antagonism between the individual and the rest is implied by the very fact of existentialism's subjectivism, from the very fact that each person is forced to pursue his own authentic life project ex-nihilo and for himself. Thus:

> Since another human being cannot be the effort of transcendence that I am, and within which I experience and give meaning to my world, he can only know me and my world in the objective mode and this knowing collapses the properly evaluative dimension of my actions and leaves them stranded as so many natural events

> awaiting another evaluative interpretation which may or may not coincide with mine.

Thus, the most common criticism levelled against existentialism from the point of view that is educationally significant is that it lacks any real social or moral explanation, and this is because existentialists are typically uncomfortable when it comes to measuring the criterion of authentic existence against the essential communality of human being. Van Cleave Morris summarizes the content of the paradox as it presents itself to the existentialist as follows, quoting from whitmarsh:

> The problem which poses is a seemingly elementary one: Is not man thrown into a world which he did not crate, confronted with obligations of a communal existence, forced to comply with the imperatives of an anonymous society, and continually faced with the inevitability of his own death-is not man, so conceived, incapable of justifying his own existence?

The existentialist argues that reason seems to drive us to answer 'Yes', to this question, but the puzzle is, says Van Cleve Morris, that this answer is, at the same time unacceptable to man; he is therefore hunted by this paradox which appears unconquerable by reason. The only response that remains to him lies in the blatant thrust beyond reason' towards a zone where values are crated in the act of an individual living a life. Morris says tat in such a situation, 'To encourage the young to invade this zone and stake out their own plots there-this is an Existentialist education.

A comparison between the characteristics of the educational theory of 'romantic' humanism, as identified by Williams and Foster, and power, and certain prominent aspects of the lifelong education literature reveals some very close similarities of viewpoint between them. With reference to the former, both sets of authors agree on its main theoretic framework such as exists, that the major influences on it come from the humanistic psychology movement of the 1960s, more particularly from the work of Rogers and Maslow whose psychotherapies are based on fulfillment theories of the personality. At the same time Williams and Foster identify within it a rationale couched in a sociological context characterised by two main factors; a stress on the rapidity of change in the environment calling for a new type of educated person able to cope with such change, and, an attempt to mitigate the effects of alienation on human beings living in technological environments. The trust of humanistic psychology in response to these twin factors is toward a theory of motivation, with an emphasis on the growth of Self-awareness as an ultimate good.

Williams and Foster further point out that, eventually, this emphasis, as is to be expected, is directed towards objectives that focus upon the self-realisation principle in life, a principle which implies that the thrust of human activities in healthy persons is towards growth, fulfillment and creativity. The principle, they say, is given its theoretical shape by Rogers, who Crystallizes his philosophy of the person as he works through therapy. In accordance with the aims of this therapy:

> The client will move away from facades; he will move away from 'oughts'; he will move away from pleasing others; he will move toward self-

> direction, toward being process, toward being complexity, toward openness to experience, toward acceptance of others and toward trust of self.

And Maslow similarly emphasises this 'auto-centered' approach, his theoretic approach being, like that of Rogers, radically subjectivist. For both, the focus is on the individual who, for good measure and consistently with naturalistic philosophies, is also regarded a priority as being essentially good and perfectible.

As in therapy, the central aim of the educational outlook of 'romantic' humanism, the authors continue, is to make the learner progressively more self-aware, more in touch with himself, his own uniquess, how he differs from others. There is therefore a centering of authority within the learner himself which, taken together with the therapeutic pedagogy implied by humanistic psychology, evidently transforms the typical role of the educator away from its traditional form. So that it actually comes to resemble that of the therapist, its central task being to develop within the learner an attitude or responsibility towards his own learning.

The lifelong education literature shares all these tendencies, beginning with the sociological context. Lifelong education theory similarly locates its own rationale and justification within societies that are undergoing change at an accelerated rate pressed on directly or indirectly by the effects of a scientific and technological revolution which has assumed the proportions of a veritable 'knowledge explosion in our times. This knowledge explosion, in turn, renders the traditional view of education as the transmission of a stock of knowledge from one generation to the next and as the forming of a stereotyped personality irrelevant. Thus the Faure report speaks about the need for a new education for a new individual, one who both understands change in its different effects and dimensions, and is able to cope with it and turn its potential to positive outcomes.

From a narrower angle than the above Power status that the common theme of 'romantic' humanism is exhibited most clearly in its criticism of traditional schooling. And this again is another clear point of similarly it shares with the lifelong education programme. One recalls among Dave's concept characteristics one that refers to the lifelong education programme as providing an antidote to the shortcomings of the existing formal education system. And the criticism goes far beyond that of historical irrelevances just referred to. In his book on Gelpi, Ireland provides a synthesized list of the objections against existent schooling recurrent in the lifelong education literature and these are, in essence, very close to the ones attributed to romantic humanists by Williams and Foster, and Power. Thus Power, for instance, says that the main charge romantic humanists level against schools is that they are little more than assembly lines perpetuating a conspiracy against individuality by accepting a commission to produce a standard product, this neglect of individuality being typically described as dehumanizing for the learner. And the same accusation is made on the side of lifelong education by Lengrand who similarly complains that no consideration is allowed in schools for individual differences of character. On the contrary pupils who do not conform to pattern become marginal, as do those whose rate of development is slowerthan the average. Moreover, he argues, the need for selection prevails over pedagogical considerations and failure is thus institutionalized at the cost of senseless wastage of intellectual and monetary investment. Education should, Lengrand says, allow every individuals to develop in accordance with his own nature and as a function of learning capacities that are his own, not in terms of ready-made models suited for one kind of personality, that of the 'gifted' pupil who learns easily and does not question the school order. Finally, and from a slightly different point of view, he charges schools, as presently organized, of resting on a turncated conception of the human personality in that the capacity to acquire knowledge is given precedence over all other terms of expression: emotional, social, aesthetic or physical. They therefore adopt a learning programme which not only has the practical effect of fragmenting the personality but also of separating the individual from life.

All these tendencies are appearing at a time when, lifelong education theorities argue, the human personality is already constantly menaacxed with 'abstraction' threatened with falling victim to elements with our contemporary civilization that conspire to divide it, to break up its unity, Lengrand is not the only one who emphasises these 'alienating' effects of the modern situation on persons, suchodolski an others do so also. In addition, however, Lengrand, like the Faure report, reportedly accuses the school of contributing greatly to the 'dissociation of the parts of the personality' which is the main symptom of this alienation. This is because, corresponding with the priority given to knowledge acquisition, the school arbitrarily isolates one aspects of the personality, the intellectual aspect in its cognitive form, as being alone educationally relevant while the other aspects are forgotten or neglected and either shrink to an embryonic state or develop in a disordered fashion; threatening the very balance of the personality. In this situation, Lengrand argues, some essential elements of the human person are actually either atrophied by schooling or else are temporarily, and even, sometimes, permanently, paralysed. While the Faure reports says:

> The neglect and disdain from which some elements of educational programmes continue to suffer, the deficiencies and imbalance of curricula appear to us to be among the most serious symptoms of the disease of which education is both the symptom and the cause. The separation of its intellectual, physical, aesthetic, moral and social components is an indication of alienation, undervaluation and mutilation of the human person.

And again we find this tendency to separate education from life similarly constitutes the grounds for serious complaints levelled against schooling by 'romantic' humanists, Couching their objections similarly in the language of 'relevance' they ask how schooling can be educationally relevant when in schools 'thought' is falsely divorced from 'life' which, they argue, is 'the crucibles of real not fictional problems. And, in any case, they insist, the question of relevance is not one that can be decided by the school since, in fact, it is really a personal one and as such requires a private verdict not a statement of policy. For these reasons there is a tendency among 'romantic' humanists to conclude that traditional schooling is largely a waste of time while, at the same time and for the most part, drawing back, like the lifelong education movement, from the inference that the whole concept of school be abolished.

The Faure report, in effect, regards the deschooling theses an 'extreme one based on the erroneous postulate that 'education constitutes an independent variable in each society. What is in question for lifelong education theorists is not whether school in itself is important of necessary, but whether it is a good thing in its current form. From this point of view the problem is not only that current schooling preserves that outworn formulae of the past but also that it continues to project the same dichotomies of the past, and there can be no remedy for this situation, lifelong education theorists hold before schools recognize that, at a time when abstract knowledge is coming to be viewed more and more as part of a continual process acting on and reacting to daily life, new solutions are required. For on such recognition depends the further recognition that the common stream of education in schools should combing theory, techniques and practice, intellectual and manual labour, The dislocation of these different combinations constitutes in concrete form the much criticized separation of education from life; its consequence in psychological terms is that the child's personality is split between tow worlds each discordant with the other: one in which it learns like a disembodied creature and the other in which it fulfills itself through some anti-educational activity. A conclusive comment on this issue is that:

> most education systems do not help their clients - whether they be youngsters or adults - to discover themselves, to understand the components of their conscious and unconscious personalities, the mechanisms of the brain, the

> operation of the intelligence, the laws governing their physical development, the meaning of their dreams and aspirations, the nature of their relations with one another and with the community at large Education thus neglects its basic duty of teaching men the art of living, loving and working in a society which they must create as an embodiment of their ideal.

Yet another point of agreement between the two sides relates to their criticism of the monopoly the school has always exercised on education. That monopoly, both argue, helps to conceal the insufficiency of what is on offer as against the real educational needs of contemporary individuals. Both, therefore, emphasise the educational importance of the wider society. Romantic humanists, rather surprisingly, insist that social interaction is the great educator; but the explanation could be that they view such interaction as a way to curb the school's pretensions. Similarly, the Faure report argues that the school must be transcended by broadening the educational function to the dimensions of society as a whole. It quotes Plutarch, in this connection, who said that the city is the best teacher, approvingly, and, of course, devotes much space to the elaboration of the principles and practices of the learning society.

Williams and Foster refer to the seven goals which Roberts has claimed to be the main ones for a humanistic education. These concern:

> personal development creative behavior, inter-personal awareness, subject orientation, specific context, method of teaching and teachers and administrators.

Roberts goals they point out, are further development by a set of imperatives designed by Fairfield to implement them in educational settings. In the context of the comparative analysis that is the object, what is especially interesting about these goals and imperatives, because they are so close in essence to those distinguished in various places by lifelong education theorists, is their provenience. They are, Williams and Foster say, inspired : by the Social Education movement, which sought to foster cooperative individualism through education; by Progressive Education, whose common principles were seen by Dewey as the expression and cultivation of individuality, free activity, learning through experience, acquiring new skills as a means to attaining ends, concentration on the here and now, and acquaintance with a changing world; and by the Open Education movement which encourages an equally active role for teacher and learner in order to develop greater classroom democracy with an emphasis on a cooperative sharing environment.

Evidently we could continue to cite other statements and positions held in common in confirmation of the fact that romantic humanism as an educational theory shares its more consistent orientations with elements in the lifelong education literature. The identification of this convergence between the two is made more consistent by their separate identification with existentialist thinking. This is not enough however to establish with any firmness the relationship of lifelong education theory itself with existentialism, nor to explain the nature of that relationship. This is the matter to which we must turn next in this section, and we can start by observing that within the lifelong education literature there is the same pronounced awareness of the psychological pressures to which people living in an environment of accelerating change are exposed, particularly when the technology is used in a socially irresponsible or malicious manner and is turned to utterly materialistic purposes, as one finds in existentialist writings. There is the same sensitivity to the dehumanizing effect of a consumeristic mass culture that is shared also by existentialist writers. Jaspers most especially, and that makes a personalized and utterly individualistic outlook appear as the only intelligible alternative to the threat of alienation posed by such a culture to the individual personality and, more especially, its sense of identity.

Reference has already been made to Suchodolski's brand of humanism. The central contention of Suchodolski's essay is that people today are faced with the threat of alienation from many sources in both capitalist and socialist countries. Lifelong education, or indeed any positive educational action, is impossible, he argues, where these conditions of alienation exist; the first strategy of the 'learning society', therefore, must be to overcome the forces of alienation within itself by reassessing its own cultural values. The existentialist, of course, with his profound distrust of collective action, does not believe this strategy possible, and a somewhat similar doubt seems to lie at the core of the thinking within the 'pragmatist' trend in lifelong education theory, which does appear to hold out hope of internal revolutions through education, but which also pins its faith in this possibility on 'progressive' individuals rather than on any form of collective action. The existentialist will respond to the threat of the modern world by emphasising the value of the personal and subjective both in terms of educational cultural action, and his counterpart among lifelong education theorists is to be found in such as Paul Lengrand, who similarly holds that Modern man is the victim of abstraction, and for whom the appropriate educational response does not focus on collective action but is similarly personalized. Lengrand, in fact, affirms the value of individuality in all its forms and per se. He argues that before the 'challenges of this age' which a highly technologized culture provokes, there are two responses open to the individual that correspond, in turn, to the existentialist's distinction between an inauthentic and an authentic existence; either passivity, an attitude of resignation and surrender, 'watching the cauldron of doctrines and beliefs without great concern over their contradictions and changes of front', or the acceptance of responsibility, the recognition of 'the obligation to be oneself'.

One thing that is clearly attractive to lifelong education theorists about existentialism is that it offers, as Lengrand's argument indicates, an ultimate justification for their programme, for it makes education the price of 'freedom' one needs to pay in a continuously challenging social milieu: 'In one sense, the modern individual is condemned to autonomy, obligated to freedom', and this obligation carries with it the price of education - 'education which never cease, which mobilises every capacity and every resource of being, whether from the intellect or from the heart and imagination'. In fact, lifelong education is made necessary for Lengrand by the fact that it is only by being in a situation where one can fight the obstacles and challenges continuously met with in a meaningful way that one is demonstrating one's humanity, and in each case the nature of the combat is a purely personal one and requires personal solutions. From this point of view, he believes that the best that the educator can do for the learner is to put him in a position where he can fend for himself, where he comes to be autonomous, and the same contention is made by the Faure report. Self-directed learning is therefore made the general aim of all formal learning by both, and indeed by all lifelong education theorists besides, who revert to the concept of 'educability' which, in turn, is translated into different conditions for the achievement of learning autonomy, which include the appropriate forms of motivation and skin, to give it form.

In effect, having rejected the view that education has primarily to do with the transmission of knowledge, or of a culture, or has anything to do with imposition of any kind, Lengrand concludes, employing an existentialist jargon, that:

> Education is not an addendum to life imposed from outside. It is no more an asset to be gained than is culture. To use the language of philosophers, it lies not in the field of 'having' but in that of 'being'. The being in a state of 'becoming' at each different stage and in varying circumstances is the true subject matter of education.

If the individual is always 'becoming' then his education, which intimately concerns his 'being in a state of 'becoming'', must always be in some sense incomplete and ongoing because the very nature of his existence demands it. The same conclusion derived from considering the nature of being is also reached from the existentialist point of view, where being is characterized by the constant need to choose, since choice is always to some extent demanded of the individual as a condition of life itself. Even in the most restrictive of circumstances, existentialists tell us, we are obliged to choose, since, however restrictive these may be, a minimal possibility of choice is always logically possible. At the same time, however, this 'formal' autonomy is meaningless because it is merely logical, it has no human or moral value. It is only the effective autonomy of authentic individual choice that has such value and is therefore of worth. It is thus that Lengrand and Suchodolski insist upon the value of 'responsibility'. It is, they say, absolutely incumbent upon the individual to take over his own cultural and educational project as the very assertion of his humanity. Thus Lengrand insists that it is vital both for the learner and for the educator to have an authentic conception of both. From the point of view of culture this amounts to an understanding that:

> A man's culture is the sum total of the efforts and experiences through which he has become steadily more himself. These efforts and experiences, even if the shares them with thousand and millions of human beings, are his own and relevant only to himself. Culture only exists to the extent to which it has been lived and tested within the particular history of a man who is leading an existence, who is building a life, who is conscious of the universe and who takes part in its shaping by his own decisions. Contrasting with this conception of culture there is another 'geographical' outlook which the individual is continuously presented with and which he needs to avoid if he is to affirm himself as a person, a culture of 'bad faith'. The 'geographical' concept of culture sees culture not as a personal possession but as a 'self-

> contained domain comprising the sum total of knowledge accumulated over the centuries'. As a domain one has the option of centering or staying outside. Moreover, once one enters one comes to occupy more of less of this territory depending on chance and other factors. Thus, the 'geographical' concept of culture divides the world into the cultural rich and the cultural poor, the privileged and the victims, the initiates and the uninitiated.

Corresponding to these different conceptions of culture, there are for Lengrand two ways in which the human phenomenon can be viewed, both of which are significant to the manner in which the educator may choose to approach education; one is the 'sociological', the other is the 'psychological' or 'philosophical'. The first, he says, is 'monopolised by the forces at work, by structures and institutions, and it is those they consider important'. The second, that which, he says, should impel educators, is:

Indeed the orientation the practice of education should take once we get these perspectives right practically suggests itself of its own accord. For, Lengrand argues, the psychological/philosophical approach clearly assumes that the aim of the educator is to help form the mind, the body and the character, and where else, he asks somewhat theoretically, do mind, body and character belong but 'within the restricted and yet limitless space of a particular individual in the context of his own being and becoming?

This individualist and auto-centered philosophy of education comes strongly across from other quarters within the lifelong education literature also. Thus we find the Faure report declaring that 'Teaching, contrary to traditional ideas and practice, should adapt itself to the learner; the learner should not have to bow to pre-established rules for teaching', and 'The new educational ethos makes the individual the master and creator of his own cultural progress', and finally, 'education is no longer focused on the learner, nor anyone, nor anything else. It must necessarily proceed from the learner'. And if we return to Cropley's defining principles of lifelong education is recognised by the UIE, referred to in earlier pages, we find the same reference to the self-fulfillment of each individual as the ultimate aim of education, and to the value of having the skill and the motivation to engage in self-directs learning activities placed above all others.

The question is, can the lifelong education programme be a straightforwardly existentialist one? One must beware not to confuse it with the different question whether existentialism can supply the basis for a lifelong education programme, which it clearly can. The issue it is meant to raise is not the latter one but whether the programme of the lifelong education movement, its operational definition in particular, as it appears in the literature, can be aligned with existentialist philosophy thus resolving the ideological ambiguities described in the giving form to the programme's humanism. It needs to be understood also that the question is about the theoretical resolvement of the programme not the practical; in other words it is about theoretical possibilities. It asks whether the programme would continue to remain internally coherent and consistent if it is aligned with existentialism, and an answer to it must have two parts; first, it must involve consideration of the difficulties brought against existentialist thought with regards to its general compatibility with educational practice - in other words, it needs to see whether the credentials of existentialism as an educational theory are right; second, it must see whether there are not any a priori objections to the attachment of the movement's programme with existentialist thought based on some conflict of defining principles between the two.

Starting with the first, there are evidently serious difficulties involved with bringing existentialist thought in general to bear on education practices, because such practices are typically assumed to involve institutional arrangements, namely the presence of schools and teachers; these, in turn, are considered indispensable in any sophisticated society for the transmission of its culture, on which its very continued existence depends. A consistent existentialist outlook, it would appear, must logically view schools or any form of collective learning within some form of institutionalized framework as undesirable. Power says:

> At best, existentialisms advice to education is vague. After adverting to existentialism's fundamental subjectivism and pluralism, not much remains on the level of philosophical principle for application to any theory of schooling.

It would also seem that existentialist thought, with its emphasis on subjectivism as the only truth, must be totally incompatible with any formal education since the latter implies the presence of an educator acting upon the learner. The discussion of the other section, in fact, raised the point that 'romantic' humanists, who are of the same theoretic temperament of the existentialists, are typically unhappy with the very concept of school, while they embrace a conception of education as a kind of therapy involving a one-to-one relationship between learner and facilitator. That they are nevertheless reluctant to throw over the concept completely accounts for their unwillingness to take over existentialist thought.

From another point of view one needs to recall the point made earlier that existentialism, with its psychological orientations, lacks a proper social philosophy; a proper theory of society. Thus while existentialists describe to us the kind of society we already have and furnish us with a phenomenological critique of the individual's existential condition within it, they nowhere tell us what, in effect, it out to be in order to improve that condition; this is because they hold an aversion for prescription or theory. In fact, as we saw earlier, the lack of any social theory in existentialist thought does not so much denote a gap, a lacuna within it, as a necessary consequent of it. The question is, can an adequate educational theory be constructed in the absence of a social philosophy?

The difficulties with conceptualizing an existentialist education programme grows when education means schooling. For if by education we mean 'school', then it is difficult to see how an existentialist philosophy can find a legitimate defense against the difficulties outlined above. For 'school' is historically a social construct, a human invention of an institutional kind which presupposes the involvement of a cooperative enterprise with shared interests and beliefs, and a shared ethic; the need for all of which the existentialist denies, and the value of which he typically rejects. But if education is understood in a wider sense then 'school' does a social philosophy continue to be required for an education programme?

Rousseau has furnished a theoretical account of how education can dispense with a social framework in Emile, while Illich and others have proposed a de-schooling philosophy. The stock reply to the former's naturalism is, however, that the social is reintroduced through the presence of Emile's tutor, while Illich replaces the school with learning networks that are 'new educational institutions'. Within a more contemporary and practical viewpoint, an increasingly large amount of adult education is being done in the Freirian manner, outside 'schools', without a formal curriculum, and with facilitators acting out therapeutic roles rather than traditional teachers - but this renders the learning situation, if anything, not less but increasingly social, and Freire's pedagogy, or and ragogy, is backed by a social analysis and an alternative philosophy. Finally, not even a social doctrine of 'authenticity' can replace a social philosophy proper, as Van Cleve Morris suggests it can do, for the very concept of an 'authentic society' where 'each individual takes personal responsibility for the law he obeys, the conventions he consents to, the values he appropriates for his own life, is as impossible as the possibility of a General Will which will always reflect in practice the views of every single member of the society whose it is, which does not demand compromise of its members, and is not sometimes prepared to 'force them to be free'.

On the other hand, societies have dispensed with schools in the past where all their specialized needs could be catered for by the training of a limited few by tutors. However, they were clearly not democratic societies, and the arrangement would most certainly fail to satisfy the increasing demands for specialized learning the characterizes all kinds of modern societies. As was pointed out earlier, Illich has suggested, theoretically, that societies can be deschooled. But again, though the suggestion is made seriously as a reaction to the effects on society which the pervasiveness of schooling engenders according to his own analysis, deschooling is not a possibility that he eventually canvasses adequately since his commendable efforts to combine individual freedom of action in learning with social cooperation must assume, in the absence of school or any formal substitute, that the ability for autonomous learning is either something one is born with or one can effectively win for oneself, or is something that can be left to peer interaction or parental guidance, and whereas the former assumption defies all evidence to the contrary, the latter leaves the child to the mercy of chance and parental good-will, which may not in itself be a bad thing in a perfect society where everybody's motives are the right ones, but not otherwise, in this imperfect world of ours where children often need to be protected from the intentions of grown ups, including their own parents.

At any rate we have already seen that lifelong education theorists do not accept the move towards deschooling society. On the contrary they are committed by their programme to a revised theory of schooling that fits with their reconceptualizing of education itself as a lifelong matter. Indeed, as we have seen, referring to the existent schooling system, one of Dave's 'concept characteristics' speaks of the lifelong education programme as an 'antidote to (its) shortcomings' rather than as a radical substitution of it, and another retains the importance of 'formal institutions of education' as 'one of the agencies of lifelong education', though not the sole one. And existentialist philosophy, as out earlier discussion showed, can contribute nothing to these designs.

However even more fundamental than its theoretical incompatibility with the concept of school, which as we have seen, is considered indispensable by the lifelong education programme, the existentialist point of view is incompatible with the very having of an educational programme, lifelong or of any other description, since any programme, even a personal one, constitutes Dave's 'concept characteristics' and the radical individualism of existentialist thought. A response to it consistent with the latter would be to avoid such exercises as Dave's. But this is not a move open to the movement. Not that, in the eventuality, it would cease to remain a movement, for movements, as was observed earlier, can admit to different degrees of cohesion, the move is not blocked on logical grounds, but that systematization is essential for policy-making, and, as we have seen, if anything unifies the lifelong education movement it is agreement over the fact, which is also considered the distinctive feature of the movement, that its conceptualization of the otherwise bare idea of education as something lasting for life includes the institutionalizing of that idea.

The fact that the lifelong education programme presupposes the need for social and political action in order to operationalize the concept also forestalls what would otherwise appear as an attractive compromise. It could be suggested that the existentialist outlook be left as a description of the adult component of the programme, with-perhaps a type of schooling that would lead to 'authenticity', that would awaken awareness in the learner—existential awareness of himself as a single subjectivity present in the world', as its other component.

Also, a connected objection to this form of compromise solution would be that, conceived of in this way, as a two-tier programme, one would be violating one of the programme's other fundamental principles, namely that within its perspective, the educational process should be viewed as a unified whole, as integrated both vertically and horizontally. In effect, a two-tier programme would simply restort to the situation current in most countries today, and to the situation in educational theory prior to the advent of the movement; before, that is, the lifelong education theorists took the bare idea that education should be for life and turned it into a programme. It would simply regard lifelong education as a purely personal project left to the perception of truly 'authentic' individuals without any social or institutional support. And this is a consequence none of the theorists within the movement would accept, for it would mean, effectively, the abrogation of the movement's programme. it would mean denying lifelong education the separate conceptual space its theorists have worked to give it within educational theory. Moreover, it would mean giving up the policy prescriptions, with which they have filled that space and denying the very case they have made for these prescriptions.

In sum, it is clear that the lifelong education programme needs to look elsewhere than towards existentialism for its philosophical statement, tough the attractions of existentialism are not to be denied, and its positive insights can still be creatively included. Among the former one could include the fact that existentialism avoids the problem of ideology by rejecting the need for one, and this makes it an attractive proposition for any who deliberately seek to avoid ideological commitment while asserting the value of individual freedom; both considerations that weight heavily on UNESCO- sponsored projects or documents. But the price to be paid for these 'advantages' is an impossible one, for theoretic consistency demands that they can be won only through the effective sacrifice of the programme itself. Indeed, there exist within the lifelong education literature strong statements to the effect that self-education is the only authentic form of education, but the fact that they coexist with further statements and with programmatic principles for the institutionalization of the concept is an indication of the looseness of the theorizing within it, or, at any rate, of the language in which it is expressed—one problem with rhetoric in fact is that it frequently contradicts itself.

On the other hand, the positive points are plenty, though they require more than careful pruning of their existentialist meanings. Indeed they need to be extracted from the whole framework of existentialism in order to bear fruit, and need to be re-introduced within a social philosophy of some kind. This means that the emphasis on individuality needs to be tempered with some account of a just system of cooperative behaviour within which the individual needs to pursue his own life project and within which the policy aspects of the education programme need to be construed. The phenomenological outlook of existentiallism gives us valuable insights into the current state of our technological civilization, which, in themselves, constitute a strong recommendation for continuing learning, but it cannot be satisfactory to define an 'authentic society' simply as one composed of authentic individuals and leave it at that. Existentialism merely tells us that a truly human existence is 'authentic', and that the 'Other' poses a threat to its pursuit, it also tells us that certain social conditions, those prevailing in modern societies, are potentially threatening to individuality. But it cannot tell us which social conditions would make authenticity is, for the existentialist, by definition, pursued against society, whatever its kind - the only answer is subjectivism.

A subjectivist educational philosophy, on the other hand, renders impossible any concept of schooling or any collective educational action - more especially the setting up of education programmes for the purposes of policy making. The subjectivist must view lifelong education as a personal thing. These are factors that render subjectivism unacceptable to the outlook of the lifelong education movement. How do other educational philosophies feature in this respect? The next chapter is a critique of liberal philosophy of education from a lifelong education perspective - it is evidently an important one given the very great influence of the philosophy.

Liberal philosophy of education

'Humanism', 'existentialism'! These are not philosophies that are particularly popular among the philosophers of education of the English - speaking world. Some description of the orientations that have characterized the outlook of these philosophers was already made. There the point was made that the overwhelming mass of contributions to Anglo-Saxon philosophy of education comes from a liberal standpoint, whether explicitly declared or thinly disguised behind a facade of 'neutrality' supported by an analytic methodology. Where an ideological debate is recognised, the 'other side' addressed is thinkers of a Marxist persuasion. The point was also made, that within liberal philosophy of education the technical definition of education used is that which includes only formal or intentional learning, the informal and non-formal being commonly considered as not counting as part of people's education, although they may be relevant and valuable for other purposes of life. Which means that liberal philosophers typically operate with a very restricted conception of education; so restricted in fact as to make education simply equivalent with schooling or with the continuation of schooling into universities and other institutions of 'higher learning.

These twin tendencies to keep education apart from 'life' and to so conceptualize education as to equate it with schooling are perfectly exemplified in an essay written by Michael Oakeshott called 'Education: the engagement and its frustration', where the major 'frustration' to education, for Oakeshott, is that of confusing it with what goes on in life, for in so doing one deprives 'School' of its most vital characteristics.

To begin from the beginning, Oakeshott defines education as:

> a specific transaction which may go on between the generations of human beings in which newcomers to the scene are initiated into the world they are to inhabit.

One needs to note the terms used and the positions the statement implies. First, we are told that education is a 'specific transaction'; i.e., it is not a 'transaction' of just any kind, but one of a certain sort. Oakeshott later specifies that what is being 'negotiated' in this transaction 'is not the transfer of the products of earlier generations to a newcomer, nor is it a newcomer acquiring an aptitude for imitating current adult human performances; it is learning to perform humanly'. One may well feel a bit puzzled as to what Oakeshott could mean by 'learning to perform humanly', and, further on, by being 'initiated into the world they are to inhabit', since a central argument of his essay is that education implies learning that is 'detach(ed) from the immediate, local world of the learner, its current concerns and the directions it gives to his attention'. But his meaning becomes amply clear when he specifies that the inheritance of human achievements and understandings into which education initiates the young is one where these are 'animated, not by the inclinations he brings with him, but by intimations of excellences and aspirations he has never dreamed of, and this is something school alone can provide, since school is the only place where the learner 'may encounter not answers to the 'loaded' questions of 'life', but questions which have never before occurred to him'. Second, there are always, says Oakeshott, at least two sides involved in any given transaction, so, education being a form of transaction, there can be no such thing as 'self education'.

Oakeshott, in fact, specifies that in education the two parties to the transaction are the newcomer or 'postulant to a human condition', and the adult as teacher. The home, the nursery and the kindegarten may be places where learning takes place, but they do not count, since such learning is usually ruled, he says, by inclination and is a by-product of play. Education, in fact, he continues, only begins with the appearance on the scene of a teacher with something important to impart which is not immediately connected with the current wants or interests of the learner:

> But education, properly speaking, begins when, upon these casual encounters provoked by the

> contingencies of moods, upon these fleeting wants and sudden enthusiasms tied to circumstances, there supervenes the deliberate initiation of a newcomer into a human inheritance of sentiments, beliefs, imaginings, understandings and activities. It begins when the transaction becomes 'schooling' and when learning becomes learning by study, and not by chance, in conditions of direction and restraint.

The 'idea of School', Oakeshott contends, is essentially that of a personal transaction between a 'teacher' and a 'learner': 'The only indispensable equipment of 'School' is teachers'. 'School' itself, on the other hand, is typically a 'monastic' institution in respect of being 'a place apart where excellences may be heard because the din of world laxities and partialities is silenced or abated'. Within the school the first lesson the newcomer learns is, therefore, that not all knowledge counts, that learning is not a 'seamless robe', the possibilities are not limitless. Thus a deliberately organized curriculum circumscribes knowledge, or the context that needs to be learnt, into 'disciplines' or 'subjects'. Moreover, school cultivates within the learner certain indispensable habits of life related to the effective 'engagement to learn by study' which becoming educated requires; habits of 'attention, concentration, patience, exactness, courage and intellectual honesty'.

Oakeshott's programme is a typical liberal one. With this fact in mind, it becomes a wonder how many liberal philosophers of education declare that they actually subscribe to the idea of lifelong education, to the extent 'that recently Anthony O'Hear has felt that he could assert that there is no controversy among philosophers over the view that education is for life; this is in fact, he says, how it is held by philosophers as far apart on other matters as Peters and Dewey. The question whether this is indeed so is one that has been tackled elsewhere in some detail; succinctly,, it can be shown the O'Hear's statement conceals fundamental discrepancies relating to how these views are held by the two philosophers, which, in effect, render the education programmes with which they work entirely different ones. Peters's position on the matter in clearly defined and succinctly stated in a statement of his in Ethics and Education in which he declares that there are at least two 'truths' contained in the 'slogan' that 'education is for life':

> One is that if people are properly educated, so that they want to go on when the pressures are off, the conceptual schemes and forms of appraisal, into which they have been initiated in schools and universities, continue to develop. Another is that 'living' cannot be separated from the ways in which people have learnt to conceive and appraise what they are doing.

In effect, when he describes the statement that 'education is for life' as a slogan, he is accurately reflecting how it is currently held in many quarters, not the least among liberal philosophers of education. For a slogan is a from of exhortation to do something. Where the 'slogan' that 'education is for life' is concerned it is a valuable on because it derives from 'conceptual truths' implied by definition from the concept of education itself, which further implies conceptual schemes and forms of appraisal into which people are initiated in schools and universities and which themselves have intrinsic value. This being the case, it follows logically that they are of a kind which it would be worthwhile to continue to develop for life. But an exhortation or recommendation, however strongly made, is not the same thing as a policy actively pursued. The fact that Petrs regard the view that 'education is for life' as a slogan demonstrates that after recommendation he would leave the matter of whether to engage in lifelong education or not up to the individual's personal initiative. He does not see lifelong education as a key idea to be further explored for its policy implications.

At this stage it is important for us to get our perspectives right. The question is not whether Peters and other liberal philosophers of education support the idea that education is for life or not, for many clearly do in some form or other. The real question is, what kind of lifelong education programme do they support? One answer is provided for us in the quotation from Peters; it is the extension of school and university learning into adult life. So, in effect, even conceived of as a lifelong matter, there is no discontinuity in Peters' statement with the view expressed by Oakeshott that education is conceptually tied with schooling; if it does not take place within the building we call school, it still involves a continuation and development of the kind of learning that goes on in the school, and, one assumes, according to definition, will continue to involve intentional learning under the guidance of teachers.

In actual fact, it may be the case with some liberal philosophers of education that they do, like O'Hear himself explains that he is writing about formal education because this suits the purposes of his book and in order to 'keep things in manageable proportions', the presupposition clearly being that formal education, or schooling is something that can be written about separately and is therefore uninfluenced by these other forms of education he has in mind and that are not formal. And Peters also, similarly acknowledges another sense of education besides that which he writes about, a sense in which it is a 'fluid concept' with a 'loose undifferentiated meaning' as compared to his own. But, like O'Hear, it is not a sense that interests him either. The point being made is that whatever other meanings they allow education, liberal philosophers are interested in one only.

Peters definers education as schooling, as do most other liberal philosophers of education,- as the initiation of the young into a form of life regarded as desirable by teachers-and this is how he writes about it. This is what really matters whatever his other statements that appear to support the idea of lifelong education may be. O' Hear himself is not even interested in verbal consistency at least. Thus he describes his intention in in his book as that of providing 'some general account of what it is we will want our children to have learned by the time their education is over. Note, 'by the time their education is over'—this from one who later says, as we have seen, that the view that education is never over is uncontroversial! We assume that, this being the case, he himself must support it! Surely that consistent statement should therefore be: 'by the time their schooling is over and they are ready to continue with their education '?! But the fact if that 'O Hear is no more aware of any inconsistecy in his position, verbal or otherwise, than is peters, Like most other liberal philosophers of education who acknowledge that education is essentially for life, both ignore this aknowledgement completely when it comes to writing about education. O' Hear is right in one sense at least for philosophical purposes, as far as he and his fellow philosophers are concerned, education is over when schooling is over, or when the aims of schooling are achieved.

Do these discrepancies mean that liberal philosophers are really paying no more than lip-service to the ideal of lifelong education? Not necessarily so. The real reason could be that the meaning of education they operate with is considered sufficient and that they would pass on to define adult or post school education simply as more of the same thing. This is what, in fact, peters appears to assume when he says that what is involved in continuing education is wanting to go on developing the conceptual schemes and forms, of appraisal into which one has already been initiated in the school . At the same time, that same meaning imposes its own restrictions on how they can consistently conceive of adult or post-school education; first because within that meaning education is something teachers do to pupils or students, and this fact, as we have said, renders the term 'self-education' and self-contradictory one in their language, second because it comprehends only a limited kind of learning and knowledge, that described by peters. The liberal philosopher does not deny that other kinds of learning are relevant or valuable in different ways, or cannot take place otherwise than through being taught or teacher directed. What he denies is that they are edecationally valuable or significant.

It goes without saying therefore that peters does not even reserve the neglected 'loose undifferentiated meaning' of education he refers to for adult hood. That adult education is, for him simply the continuation of school learning is, as we have seen, something he practically expresses explicity. But would he want to continue to be consistent to the extent of retaining that a teacher needs to be involved for education to take place? We cannot be sure, but what is certain is that many liberal philosophers of educational ideal. They would therefore, probably, want to answer no, because a successful schooling aimed towards autonomy will have given the individual the skills as well as the motivation to go it alone afterwards, thereby making tutelage unnecessary. At the same time such a view could consistently allow that educational relevance of non-formal learning, providing that what is being developed through its activities is the conceptual schemes and formes of appraisal appropriate to the study of the disciplines, not something else, thereby preserving continuity with the school. If we consider this programme as 'educational for life' it cannot evidently be called a lifelong education programme since, to be properly so called. peters and the other liberal philosophers would also have to fall in with lengrand's condition that educational value be conceded to infant learning. Its proper name would be continuing education.

All of this, however, does cinsiderable violence to the original liberal technical definition of education, since all it keeps constant from that definition is the knowledge condition, otherwise it drops the condition that learning must be formal and that it requires the direction of teachers, although continuity could also be claimed with the latter in an extended sense in which the learning to be continued started with a teacher. Such a programme would leave the matter of adult education entirely to individual initiative, since, on the one hand it is evidently unthinkable that education should continue the work of teachers and schools as liberal philosophers identify it- these are the universities and the other formal tertiary establishments, attendance at which is voluntary.

It is clear that in order to proceed to the kind of programme sketched in the last paragraph of the previous section liberal philosophy of education would need to effect important departures from its present outlook. First, it would be necessary for liberal philosophers to recognize that their initial definition of education conceived of in broader terms than childhood. Second, they will need to concede the relevance of non-formal learning to the practice of education. Otherwise they can evidently continue to insist that only teacher-guided learning is education and that education cannot be pursued outside institution or outside some form of tutorship, which is not, if we read them rightly, what most liberal philosophers intend, though it is a theoretical possibilities of their education programme. On the other hand a broader liberal programme could, as was suggested earlier, continue to hold the knowledge conditions that characterize that liberal outlook and, evidently, liberal political ideology, constant. It would than be possible to assume that these consistent with other forms of learning than the teacher-based though it could be conceded that teacher-based learning, especially in its characteristic form as schoolling, is indispensable to set the ball rolling. The context of education, then, from the point of view of a continuing education programme, would not necessarily be the school, but any locus of individual cooperative,or tutor/teacher led learning which achieves for the individual the kind of knowledge and 'mental development' in terms of which liberal education is defined, at any time in life.

This solution appears deceptively simples: in fact it is not. For besides the changes proposed one would need to effect another one of an even more radical kind: it would be necessary for liberal philosophers to discard number of concepts and emphases that are current in liberal philosophy of education and that constitute an obstacle to reconceptualizing education in this way. And this proposal appears to be the most difficult to pursue, in fact it does not seem currently possible. This is because the necessary presupposition for it to happen is a prior cognition on the part of the liberal philosophers themselves, or the fact that a femlly consistent view of education as something that continues for life requires the reassessment of their educational outlook in the manner described above or in other ways. And this awareness, as was argued in the previous section, currently appears nowhere, since almost all these philosophers continue to hold their declared support for lifelong education against a theoretical outlook which restricts education to childhood and formal learning within schools, blissfully unaware of any inconsistency on their part.

We say almost because in fact the point is taken by Jone White who devotes a whole section to lifelong education, which he correctly characterizes as a challenge to the liberal education programme to which he himself subscribes. White recognized the argument made above. He also recognizes that what is currently being proposed in name of lifelong education is a much more radical reapprais al of education even than that outlined above. White recognizes that the lifelong education programme demands a total reconceptualization of the whole of education rather than these limited corrective measures. His concern in his book however is not to contribute to the discussion of how the liberal programme can be better alingend withthe concept of lifelong education program,me demand a total reconceptualization of the whole of education rathe than these limited corrective measures. his concern in his book however is not to contribute to the discussionof how the liberal programme can be better aligned with the concept of lifelong educaiton, but to reject the concepty on behalf of liberal educaton. And in the process he evidently lights upon the spots where the inconsistencies between the two are most pronounced. In doing so he highlights the concewpts and emphases the current liberal programme would need to discard in order to achieve compatibility withthe concept of lifelong education -althouth, evidently, he does not advocate that it should do so, taking the inconsistencies, on the contrary, as reasons for rejecting lifelong education.

White's attack on the lifelong education concept takes different forms: he argues that the concept violates and renders meaningless the central concept of liberal philosophy of education; the concept of the educated man or person; he argues that it removes the emphasis from childhood. which no longer remains special from the educational point of view; he argues that it can be reduced and absurdum. All of these are meant as serious objections made by a serious philosopher, and therefore need to be met; they are also objections that do not appear elsewhere in philosophy of education. White's section, in fact, constitutes the only real philosophical critique of the lifelong education concept available at the time of writing this book, and the fact, that it is made from a hostile or, more accurately, sceptical position, renders it additionally important. It will therefore be considered in some detail in the pages to come, beginning with the problem he raises over the incompatibility of the lifelong education concept with that of the educated man.

with reference to it, white says:

If education is to be reconceptualized as a

> lifelong process and not as something belonging only to youth, then we might as well drop the concept of the educated man: there is no line to be crossed; the journey goes on for ever.

And he evidently thinks the concept so crucial that it should be guarded against this eventuality.

The reasoning behind this viewpoint goes something like this: being an intentional activity guided by set of aims of some kind. That aim or set of aims or some kind. That aim or set of aims must reflect qualities that it is desirable that people should have and that their education should give them; we call the individual who acquires these qualities an 'educated person'. The educated person, then, is one who possesses certain qualities that are deemed desirable and that are achieved through education; he can be described as the embodiment of the aims of education. The language of aims is thus an important one for the liberal philosopher of education and he is ready to pursue its logic. The language of aims is the language of deliberate action, the language of 'targets' to be aimed at; to have an aim means to have a target in focus on which one can adjust one's sights. When the language of aims is pursed further in connection with education the analogy immediately presents itself; education is a set of end results towards which teachers direct their pupils with specific criteria of achievement in mind. The latter is understood within the terms of the analogy itself since one cannot properly be said to be aiming at something without the understanding that one also knows what it means to hit it, how a successful aim shows itself. To pursue the analogy a little bit further, just as success in hitting the target closes off the action begun by aiming at it, so education is closed off when the aims of education have been achieved and one has acquired the qualities of the educated person. But this whole language game cannot be played if one introduces into it the alien concept of lifelong education; because the concept renders the conclusion we have just reached paradoxical. For if a person is educated, then the aim of education has been reached; as far as he is concerned his education is completed, the line has been crossed - whatever learning lies beyond cannot be his continuing education.

The language of liberal philosophy of education is oriented in this way; it recognizes the ultimate purpose of educating people as being that of achieving for them the characteristic of educatedness as they are identified by liberal philosophy. With particular reference to White he in fact describes his own clearly stated set of educational aims, his set of qualities of the educated man or person, and distinguishes them from those of other liberal philosophers of education by the fact that while the latter focus on the knowledge conditions, in the main, he himself focuses on virtue. His concept, therefore, he says, avoids that over-emphasis on the cognitive which has rendered liberal conceptions of educatedness the object of so much criticism. At the same time, and in conformity with our previous exposition of the liberal argument, educatedness is for him, as it must be with all the other liberal philosophers of education, a point of arrival, like stepping into a new state. It is for this reason that the need for a demarcation line which will mark it our presents itself for him. And he finds it necessary to dedicate some pages to the unenvious task of trying to sort out the question of where the line lies. His conclusion is, in fact, that it cannot be defined very specifically:

> This is partly because there are no sharp lines, only blurred areas, in anybody's case, and partly because people learn at different rates and some may be slower than others in reaching the blurred areas. Some may never reach it, although we may still want to call them partially educated, since they have travelled some way along the same road as others.

But, in any case, a person is 'more or less educated':

> when he has formed something like a coherent life plan in the light of all the considerations built into the substantive account of educational aims presented earlier, and is aware of the kinds of future circumstances which might cause him to adjust his valuations as he goes through life.

So, there are no sharp demarcation lines that mark off the point of arrival that is educatedness, only 'very blurred areas' that individuals will reach at different times in their lives and that some people may never reach at all since it is clear that not everybody will be able at any stage in his life to reach the condition where his life appears to him as a coherent life plan fulfilling 'all the considerations built into the substantive account of educational aims' that white distinguishes. Few people, in fact, will ever be 'something of a philosopher', which is what, ultimately, he expects the educated man to be, although he recognizes the merits of those who can only ever manage part of the journey.

At the same time, this very indeterminacy in establishing where the demarcation line into educatedness lies, and White's own unwillingness to close the fruits of education off for the individual arbitrarily before these have been achieved, because of their very value, renders him reluctant to take any age as a 'cut-off point', though he does insist that educatedness may be achieved, indeed ideally should be achieved by the end of schooling, since one's schooling should have turned one into an educated man. But the fact that with many it will not have done so and that some at least will arrive later means that the possibility of educatedness must be kept permanently open, though, as White perceives 'a logical gap immediately open up between aims and terminal school objectives', on this account.

The question is, how does he respond to the perception of this gap? The logical way would seem to be that of holding up continuing education as a back up for those who have been unfortunate enough to have failed to achieve educatedness at school - this would turn it into a species of compensatory programme for a defective schooling. In fact White suggests something of the kind but he warns us not to confuse it with lifelong education:

We might then envisage compulsory full-time schooling until say 16 or later, possibly followed by compulsory part-time education for another period, with strong official encouragement to continue one's education on a voluntary basis beyond this point. This would not be 'lifelong' education, since the overall objective would only be to produce educated persons and this might be achievable while people are still young.

True, this programme would not be lifelong education, but it would not be 'upbringing' either.

This is in fact how White, like most other liberal philosophers of education, defines education, as 'upbringing'. And, evidently, the consequence of so defining it is to tie the concept specifically with that of childhood. Education, as upbringing, is something that older people, notably teachers, do to the younger. So the obvious question, with regard to the programme White outlines above, is, how is this definition compatible with it? How does one continue with one's education on a voluntary basis beyond full-time schooling if education equals up-bringing? Moreover, White emphasises the fact that, as upbringing, education has nothing to do with the will or desire of the educand. This is because upbringing necessarily implies compulsion: children do not decide whether they want to be brought up or not - their upbringing is both a non-voluntary and a necessary thing. This is because, as O'Hear points out, there are certain kinds of knowledge and certain dispositions that it is desirable children should have when they grow up, and it appears that having them cannot wait. Among these perhaps the most important, from White's point of view, are dispositions of a moral kind, the 'main girders' of which need to be put in place in childhood.

From the point of view of lifelong education, however, the problems with defining education as upbringing are evident. On the one hand restricting upbringing to childhood, as liberal philosophers do, and defining education as upbringing renders it contradictory to describe education as a lifelong process; of education happens in childhood then it becomes incoherent to refer to it as lifelong. If, on the other hand, we keep the formula education equals upbringing and propose to consider the former as lifelong, notwithstanding, we can only be, consistently with this definition, proposing lifelong upbringing. This latter conclusion is, in fact, the one White would consistently be committed to if he wishes to keep the programme described about together with his definition of education as upbringing - it is the only way in which he can consistently close the gap.

So if space is to be found for the view that education is a life long process within the liberal programme, a considerable amount more will be involved than the philosopher's pious approval of it as a truism and a recommendable slogan. The fact is, as White's difficulties with the concept show, the liberal paradigm is not so conceived as to absorb it; it operates with a language game that makes it s inclusion paradoxical, mainly because it is a language game focused upon the understanding that education denotes some kind of upbringing that leads to a state of educatedness, and bringing somebody up is an intentional activity with finite and well-defined results that are ascertainable. In other words the task of adapting the liberal education programme to absorb the principle of lifelong education is a much more formidable one than may appear to be the case at first glance.

We have seen that White is right in claiming that the concept of lifelong education does not go with that of the educated man. But while this means that a liberal programme that focuses on the latter cannot accommodate the former, it is not itself a criticism of the former, it is simply the statement of a fact, tantamount to statement that 'X is incompatible with Y', no more. The question why Y should be retained in preference to X is a totally different one, in our case it is the crucial one, but it is not one that White even attempts to tackle. It is only by showing in a decisive way the necessity of retaining the concept of the educated man. by showing, for instance, that the language of education itself is rendered incoherent in the absence of such a concept, that one can object on philosophical grounds to any reconceptualizing of education that does away with it; and this is something White does not do. He seems to assume that the concept is required but he does not argue for it.

This, however, is clearly insufficient. All the more so since he would, in fact, be quite pressed to offer a defence of the current concept of the educated man from attack from some quarters within liberal philosophy of education itself. For instance from the kind of objections brought against it in Jane Roland Martin's essay on 'The Ideal of the Educated Person'.

The specific target of Roland Martin's attack is in fact Peters' concept of the educated man, but she makes it clear that here objections are equally applicable to other similar conceptions that differ from that of Peters only in detail; Downie, Loudfoot and Telfer's, for instance, and that of Woods and Barrow, as she herself indicates. Her first objection is to the expression 'educated man' itself. What is at issue, she points out, is not a simple matter of nomenclature; the question is a much more serious and substantial one than that. For, drawing on an impressive bulk of feminist research, Roland Martin makes the startling claim that the term itself is, in fact, accurate because Peters' model is sexist; so the problem is not a terminological one but a conceptual one. It is 'sexist', she argues, because, for one thing, it describes the process of becoming educated as that of being initiated into the existing forms of knowledge or disciplines, and these, she says, clearly 'incorporate a male cognitive perspective'.

> the intellectual disciplines into which a person must be initiated to become an educated person exclude women and their works, construct the

> female to the male image of her and deny the truly feminine qualities she does possess.

Coincides with our cultural stereotype of a male human being. According to the stereotype men are objective, analytic, rational; they are interested in ideas and things that have no interpersonal orientation; they are neither nurturant nor supportive, neither emphathetic nor sensitive. According to the stereotype, nurturance and supportiveness, empathy and sensitivity are female attributes. Institution is a female attribute too.

This means, Roland Martin says, that in confrontation with Peters' conception of being educated women are put in a 'double bind': 'To be educated they must give up their own way of experiencing and looking at the world, thus alienating themselves from themselves'. And this fact effectively puts them in a 'no-win situation', for, to begin with, it is a priori more difficult for women to succeed on terms that are so heavily loaded in favour of men. Moreover, even if they do succeed in acquiring the qualities of educatedness described by the model, women do so at a price which is not demanded of men and which is far from insignificant; that of denaturalizing themselves. Furthermore, Roland Martin continues, the emotional suffering entailed by having to pay such a price is augmented by the fact that even if a woman does acquire the traits characterized by the ideal, these are appraised negatively by others, notably by men themselves. So that, in effect, a liberal curriculum that objectifies the educated man, or person, more often than not the difference is only a matter of nomenclature, as its ultimate aim puts a woman in a position where, if she 'has acquired the traits of an educated person will not be evaluated positively for having them, while one who has acquired those traits for which she will be positively evaluated will not have achieved the ideal'.

These objections cannot themselves be dismissed lightly, and Roland Martin adds to them from an even broader and inclusive perspective. She argues that, as we have seen, not only is the current liberal ideal of the educated person damaging to women, it is also'far too narrow to guide the educational enterprise' in another significant manner, which makes it not fitting for men either. For the model which embodies it is too heavily biased towards the cognitive, to the extent that 'it presupposes a divorce of mind from body, thought from action, and reason from feeling and emotion', it therefore 'provides at best an ideal of an educated mind, not an educated person'. Further, this same bias on an utterly individualist one which eschews any kind of social orientation for education goals: 'Concern for people, and for interpersonal relationships has no role to play: the educated person's sensitivity is to the standards immanent in activities, not to other human beings.

Finally, Roland Martin says, the model deliberately, and again to the disadvantage of woman, rules out what she calls the 'reproductive' social functions from the concept of educatedness. She argues that Peters' conception of the educated person: in fact, whatever its pretensions, is a 'functionalist' one: 'he assigns to education the function of developing the traits and qualities and to some extent the skills of one whose role is to use and produce ideas'. Thus, for the model to be sufficiently broad, 'the two kinds of societal processes which Peters divorces from one another must be joined together'.

White, who uses the term 'educated man' throughout his book, does, to some degree, succeed in avoiding some of this criticism. Sensitive to the overemphasis on the cognitive which all the other models display, he makes, as we have seen, virtues more central than knowledge in his own model. Thus, the educated man, White says, 'is someone who has come to care about his own well-being in the extended sense which includes his living a morally virtuous life, this latter containing a civic dimension among others'.

To some degree only because White's Aristotelian model of virtue is utterly rationalist; his virtuous man is one who is 'knowledgeable in all sorts of ways'. Moreover, though being knowledgeable may not be 'a self-justifying state on its own', still 'knowledge is necessary to virtue', and the forms of knowledge virtue requires 'are indeed complex and extensive', so that the virtuous man needs, as 'something of a philosopher', to be 'able and prepared to think things through without falling into obscurity or blindly taking over the pronouncements of authority'. In short, we are practically back where Peters started with regards to the traits, characteristics and skills of being educated, what changes with white's model is its orientation towards the civic, and while the importance of this change needs to be acknowledged it does not itself nullify the other ctiticism contained in Roland Martin's essay.

It is important to note that Roland Martin herself does not recommend that the concept of educatedness or of the educated person be abandoned. What she demands is that it be broadened in different ways; in the first place to include 'experience and activities that have traditionally been considered to belong to women'. also to include the 'hidden curriculum'. and so on. In other words what she wants in a redefined liberal programme which takes in these omissions and which does not draw too sharp a line between certain 'logical and contingent relationships'; between the results of conceptual analysis and 'the contingent relationships which obtain between them and both the good life and the good society'.

Because of this proposal to broaden considerably the concept of the educated person which Roland Martin makes, she finds herself constrained at one point to raise the question 'whether we should adopt one or more ideals of the educated person'. But she leaves it undiscussed. And yet it is an important question for it seems to entitle the further question whether it is useful, on her description, to retain a concept of the educated person at all if it is going to be multiplied in several different ways. Moreover, once one advocates the having of a multiplicity of ideals one raises complications making it difficult to specify what the aims of teaching should be in such a situation. The implication is clearly that reaching should, in this light, have different aims, but this suggestion clearly starts a train of consequences that would takes us right out of the liberal education programme into something quite different.

The second major problem White sees with the concept of lifelong education is, as we have said, its conflict with our usual way of identifying education with childhood. We have seen how he himself defines education as upbringing, with the additional comment that this is in fact how it is defined by the majority of liberal philosophers of education. And, White argues, this is just since 'Whatever else happens there must be some sort of preparation for life in any society'. So the first argument for defining education as upbringing is that the bringing up of the young is necessary in any kind of society, that upbringing is a necessary phase of life both for the individual and for society itself and that it is therefore something no society can possibly ignore or leave to chance and therefore needs to institutionalize in a formal matter as education. White also presents a variation to this argument. Education, he says, belongs specifically to youth because 'the main girders of the kind of education I am recommending will have to be put in place in the early years'. This argument presents a somewhat different twist from the first; White is here making a case for the priority of youth because his own programme requires it.

Neither objection however appears to carry much force against conceptualizing education as lifelong. The first appears particularly fragile because there is nothing about a reconceptualized view of education as a lifelong process that a priorl precludes a due recognition of the sort of preparation White indicates, or, more generally, denies the relevance of upbringing, indeed the more usual offenders in this respect are his fellow liberal philosophers of education who draw sharp conceptual distinctions between the sort of upbringing that counts as education and 'socialization'. The lifelong education programme itself stipulates only that there needs to be continuity between the different phases or stages of the individual's development, it does not deny the need to consider the defining characteristics of each different stage and give it due with. On the contrary, the particular needs of each stage, and the demands made on it by society are considered within the programme to be educationally important. The programme does not, in sum, deny the fact or value of upbringing, what it refuses to do it is define education as upbringing, and that is a different thing.

The second is similarly weak because it appears to assume that there can be no viable alternative to White's programme and that, therefore, incompatibility with it is a conclusive objection against any educational viewpoint not only the lifelong education one. In fact, this is substantially the same argument as that presented earlier, where the concept of lifelong education was rejected on the grounds of its incompatibility with the concept of the educated person. The same kind of response can therefore be made to it; White is merely making the point that the view that education is a lifelong process does not go with its definition as upbringing, just as it does not go with a concept of educatedness, any more.

At the same time his concern that conceptualizing education as a lifelong process would cause us to neglect placing the 'main girders' of his education programme in youth arises from a just observation. This is that conceptualizing it in this way means removing education's traditional focus on youth and thereby reducing the relation between upbringing and adult learning to one of mere co-equivalence. This is in fact true, the concept of lifelong education implies this consequence. Not only that, the advocates of lifelong education actually tend to focus more strongly on adult education than youth. But this is only to redress the current imbalance in question to be asked is whether the latter imbalance still a good think to focus education on youth and upbringing. Lifelong education theorists argue that it is not, and they present their case accordingly. At the same time they would agree with white that there are certain 'girders' that need to be placed in youth, though they would opt for a different set of girders that his in indentifying the kind of knowledge that should be focused on in upbringing. They would, infact, support the case for educability as against initiation into forms of intrinsically valuable knowledge as the focus of formal learning. How, on thė other hand, they would focus their moral objectives, is a question that admits of different answers though, as will be argued later, a particular kind of socialization is implied by the normative statements in the lifelong education literature.

The important point to be made in clarification of White's objection is that the lifelong education programme de-emphasizes the prominence of youth not by downgrading its importance but by upgrading the education importance and value of adulthood. So the case White needs to make is against upgrading the educational importance and value of adulthood if he wants to reject conceptualizing education as lifelong.

White, however, finds still further cause for disquiet with the lifelong education programme besides. We have already mentioned the fact that, for him, tying education up with upbringing makes it a matter coorcion rather than voluntary will. White shows concern that thinking of education as lifelong or as 'a way of life' may 'blur the vital distinction between a person's upbringing, which for him cannot be voluntary. The problem that such 'blurring' may serve to obliterate the since qua non nature upgrading has already been considered and seen to be unreal. The problem now raised returns us to the problem of the logical gap between achieving educatedness and the terminal objectives of school raised, as we have seen, by White himself. It was pointed out in fact that in accordance with his programme, the only logically consistent was to close the gap is to conceptualize the continuing learning which her proposes as continuing learning which he proposes as continuing upbringing. And whil: he appears to be unconcious of this consequence where his own position is concerned, he seems very much aware of its critical possibilities with regards to the lifelong education programme and warns that the countervailing argument for liberty education beyond childhood. Nevertheless he feels continuing education as far as he thinks permissible. Thus we have already seen that he envisages the possibility of 'compulsory part-time education' for a period beyond schooling, and would give strong official encouragement, for those who are inclined to continue voluentarily beyond. It is interesting to seen what he has in mind by 'encouraement'.

This goes a little further than saying that post-compulsory provision should exist on a voluntary basis. It could mean, for instance, providing incentives in time or money for young workers to undertake educational courses or to pursue their own self-educational courses or to pursue their own self-education. It could mean reshaping conventional social expectations via the media, for instance, so that becoming educated in a full sense becomes the done thing. It could mean not only strengthening and making more accessible those agencies career guidance units, marriage counselors, almoners, Gingerbread groups, Cruse, psychiatric services and also on which help people to reflect on the shape of their lives as a whole, but also reconceptualizing them as educational agencies. Looked at this way, the period of compulsory education would have the function of laying the groundworlk for a coherent life-plan, with strong encouragement for the individual after this period to reconsider and revise this life-plan with help from formal informal agencies, if necessary.

But a feeling of confusion on reading this important

passage is natural—White himself has apparently elaborated a perfectly coherent programme of continuing education, expanding upon the principles outlined before. But when he refers to young workers undertaking education accuses or pursuing their own self-education, now is he using the term 'education' does he still mean to refere to it as upbringing? Clearly not, for the term 'self-upbringing' is a contradictory one. On the other hand, the term 'self-education, how is he using the term education, does he still mean to refer to it as upbringing? Clearly not, for the term self-upbringing is a contradictory one. On the other hand, the term self-education should be even feature in White's language game. And when he refers to the possibility of recomceptualizing the various agencies he mentions as educational agencies des he mean that their aims are set for them by the aims of education entailed by the concept of educatedness and ideally already attained in the school? Or is he operating with a different, wiser, meaning of education as something which 'help(s) people to reflect on the shape of their lives as a while ? Naturally, the inconsistencies become more glaring once the programme is elaborated further, nor is this fact lost on White. In fact, he realizes that an education programme of this kind poses problems for him.

But, even more serious as far as he is concerned, is the fact that what appears to push him, nevertheless, in its direction is the apparent implication of a concept which he evidently considers crucial to his own description of educatedness, to his own education programme the concept of life plan. We have seen how having an integrated lifeplan. We have seen how having an integrated life plan of a certain kind is, for White, the sure sign of being educated. He now poses himself the following problem if being educated means being in possession of an integrated lifeplan, it may still be argued that a person's life plan is always subject to change as life itself forces us to re-evaluate and change our priorities. This being the case it may be contended that a person's life plan is never fully settled and therfore his education, in my sense, must go on throughout his life. The only satisfactory upbringing is lifelong education. In order words White seems to be condensing, as indeed he must, that logic and his own description of educatedness drive him towards a view of education as a lifelong process, and this is indeed a catastrophic suggestion as for as the coherence of his own programme is concerned to say that although there is a lot which is true and important in this argument it is nevertheless an exaggeration for it would he says, for instance, imply that the 80-year-old man who is readjusting his priorities in the light of old age still has not completed his upbringing.

The feeling that would appear legitimate at this point is one of desperation. For it is so evident, so patently clear that the reduction in this argument depends upon the illicit interchangeability of the two terms education and upbringing that it is a real wonder that white does not see it. Observe, his education etc. The only satisfactory upbringing etc. and there is something absurd about the view that an 80-year-old has no complete his upbringing. True, but there is nothing absurd about the view that an 80-year-old man has not yet complete his education, particularly if he still has the capability of readjusting his priorities, and we do not think that White would want to deny it. Indeed, he could not consistently deny it, for did he not himself hold that there is no cut-off point for the achieving of educatedness? surely this position in itself should have demonstrated to him the nonsense of making education and upbringing one and the same thing. But apparently it has not. Or is it because it is only by to-ing and fro-ing in this way between the two terms that he can win his point that he continues to appear blind to it ? Surely he cannot really think that this argument about the 80-year-old man lets him off the conclusion he is so desperate to avoid !

Indeed what the argument shows up is not the absurdity of conceptualizing education as a lifelong process but the absurdity of defining education as upbringing, because so defined it clearly cannot stand for all the things we want to apply it to or say on its behalf, It does not even suit, as he himself is in practice forced to concede, White's own account of education, and this not merely because of the implications of including within it the concept of a life plan, but also because that account is such that within it he wants to hold that one's education can and with many people will, need to go on beyond one's upbrining even if education is conceived of as the achievement of educatedness.

Finally, any a priori uncertainty over the moral implications of holding that education is lifelong only exists it education is defined as upbringing. For, if it is, then it is clearly not only absurd to hold that an 80-year-old should continue with his education, it is also clearly immoral, given the logic of the term upbringing as described earlier, and countervailing right to freedom for adults which White cities., If we, however, refuse the definition them there in no problem particularly if by further implication, we thereby include non-formal agencies and activities within out alternative, broader, conception of education. There are places in white's book, not least in the lengthy quotation reproduced earlier, where he does operate with Vjpa broader meaning of education because this alone will suit his purposes. Surely then, on balance and all things considered it appears more worthwhile for his to abandon his definition of education as upbringing rather than continue to hold on to it, especially if he price to be paid otherwise is either to live with the inconsistencies brought to light in these pages, or the abandonment of all that has been shown to be inconsistent in his own position with the definition.

This chapter has considered the different problems relative to the compatibility of the lifelong education concept and what it entails, and the liberal education programme as it is rationalized by liberal philosophers of education. No need to devote a separate chapter to a similar comparison of the concept with the orthodox Marxian programme is felt because there are no real fundamental differences between Marxists and liberals over the technical definition of education that guides their respective programmes both conceptualize education in formal terms and more narrowly, tend to identify it with schooling. Thus, as is well known, Marx himself wrote very little specifically about education, though many of the concepts he explored in his social philosophy have been utilized in educational theory, while Gramsci who, of all the Marxist thinkers, was perhaps the most interested in the subject, while similarly contributing concepts from his broader political writings, like that of hegemony for instance, to educational discourse, was extraordinarily conservative where his explicit contributions to education are made. For the most part Marxist philosophers have been content to criticize the liberal education programme for the values it rationalizes through its curriculum and for its contribution towards the liberal - capitalist status quo, otherwise they has retained the same focus and, basically, the same emphases, in some cases substituting the concept of the class-based organic intellectual perhaps for that of the educated person.

With reference to the liberal philosophers of education, we have seen that they are, for the most part perhaps, ready to concede the view that education is for life in the temporal sense of the expression, but that they also, at the same time, define it as something formal, involving teachers and continuting, education programme would quite simply encourage people o continue to develop what has been achieved in schooling on a personal basis. White, who has taken up the question more specifically, unlike Peters whose contribution is a mere passing comment, would agree partially and with important reservations. For, he points out, the scope of such a programme must continue to be the achievement of educatedness, therefore, logically, once this is achieved for any particular person, his education is completed. There will therefore be a number of people who will not need lifelong education is completed. There will therefore be a number of people who will not need lifelong education because their journey will have been completed early on in life, ideally by the end of school. The only concession to the concept of lifelong education then that white makes in his books referes to a continuing compensatory leaning for those who need it. It is impossible to ascertain how far Peters would be in accord with this conclusion, but White in certainly right in insisting that this is not the proposal of a lifelong education programme since its lifelong expression is a concession to failure not an ideal.

At the same time White has shown most clearly

where the problem of achieving compatibility between the liberal programme and the concept of lifelong education lies. He has shown that reconceptualizing education as a lifelong programme inevitably violated certain key concepts retained to be indispensable by liberal philosophers, notably that of educatedness or of the educated person, it also challenges the liberal tendency to define education as upbringing. In the chapter we have not made a specific list of the points of contrast between the liberal programme and the movement's lifelong education programme, which are evidently numerous himself. What we have said is that a liberal continuing education programme could continue to rationalize the traditional schooling aims and activities and define its continuing component as the extension of these aims and activities in time, providing it abandons the concept of educatedness. Some further modifications to the original programme, though by no means minor in themselves, may, it is suspected, also meet with the approval of many liberal philosophers in order to give the continuing programme more breadth and freedom, the main ones would be the removal of the conditions that education requires the participation to teachers, which would allow the concept of self education, and that it typically takes place in school and similar institutions.

A total reconceptualisation of education as a lifelong programme, on the other hand, would, as White shows, require even more radical modifications than these, it would require a completely different theatre of discussion, a completely different theatre of discussion, a completely new language paradigm the bringing into operation of which would effectively entail the very abandonement of the current liberal education programme. The question to be addressed once it is accepted that the key concepts to be abandoned are not indispensable to an intelligible description of education, is, how consistent would this reconceptualized programme be with liberal social and political philosophy how consistent would it be with the ideological core of the liberal education programme? The question is a substantially different one from that which faces us when we inquire into the possibility of an existentialist lifelong education programme, where the problems, as we have seen arise from the very unwillingness of existentialist though to present itself as a programme, and from the fact that there is no real ideological core to existentalism as a philosophy.

No more than a cursory glance through the literature is require to establish that the ideological focus of the liberal education programme is the concept of personal autonomy this is considered by most liberal philosophers to be the highest political good. The focus on autonomy, on the other hand, encourages an individualist educational philosophy, and several liberal philosophers have carried the individualist orientation so far as to draw sharp conceptual distinctions between education as the development of mind and socialisation which is the turning of individuals into current men. To this extent they have shown the same diffidence towards the social as that shown by existentialist thinkers. At the same time they have typically stopped short of pitching their ideal of autonomy is something people need to be educated into. They have thus avoided holding aims that, when translated educationally, are incompatible with schools should avoid indoctrinating people. This they can do by concentrating on initiating pupils into forms of knowledge that are intrinsically valuable in morally unobjectionable ways that eventually lead to the liberating of the mind. This is the paradigm that dictates how upbrining is to be conceived. And White, who shares all these views, continues to emphasise the difference between autonomy and the existentialist's authenticity by stressing that being autonomous implies having a coherent life plan nor making criterionless choices; it is thus that autonomy, unlike authenticity, can be made the object of education.

8

Educational Theory and Its Relation to Educational Practice

Whatever subtle nuances of meaning it may have for educational theorists, for educational practitioners 'theory' is something to be regarded with suspicion and mistrust. 'Theory' is opposed to 'practice' and that very opposition is usually enough to arouse expectations of irrelevant jargon which has nothing to do with everyday practical problems and concerns. Over the years, educational theorists have made strenuous efforts to overcome this kind of antagonism, but all the signs suggest that they are making little progress. Despite our best intentions, the gap between theory and practice stubbornly remains.

As somebody who works at the 'theory' end of the education business, I naturally find this situation hard to accept. At the same time, though, I also believe that it is based on a misunderstanding which has impeded the development of a proper relationship between theorists and practitioners for a long time: the twin illusion that some people 'theorize' about education without any concern for how it is practised, while others 'practise' education with any concern for how it is theoretically to be studied or understood. This is an illusory understanding of the theory-practice relationship because there is no one set of concerns about how to engage in educational practice. To hold a view about educational theory is also to hold a view about educational practice. It follows from this that questions about educational practice and questions about educational theory are always closely related. It also follows that contentious arguments about the nature and role of educational 'theory' are, at one and the same time, contentious arguments about the nature and role of educational practice.

In this chapter I want to substantiate this general claim by providing a highly compressed historical outline of the evolution of educational theory in the twentieth century. I do this to show how the different versions of educational theory now available to us are not just the product of a series of abstract methodological arguments about the nature of 'theory'; they also reflect changes in our way of thinking about educational practice as well. My hope is that this kinds of historical understanding of different forms of educational theorizing will make it easier to reveal the different conceptions of educational practice each incorporates.

Throughout much of the nineteenth century, teachers acquired their training in a demonstration school under the supervision of a Master or Mistress of Method. Towards the end of the century, as the provision of elementary education expanded, it was felt that this 'apprenticeship' method of teacher training was no longer adequate and that, as well as learning practical teaching skills, prospective teachers should also acquire some knowledge of 'theory'. One influential educationalist, writing in 1884, put the point like this:

What English Schoolmasters now stand in need of is theory, and, further, that the Universities have special advantages for meeting this need.

As this opinion carried the day and teacher education moved into universities, so courses in 'Educational theory' began to proliferate. These courses reflected a conventional assumption of the times: that educational theory was essentially a form of philosophical enquiry concerned to raise fundamental questions about the nature of education and its relationship to society through a philosophical study of knowledge, human nature, and the good for man. In practice, however, the kind of educational theory courses that actually appeared did not so much raise fundamental questions as give potted accounts of the answers provided by various historically influential philosophers. Writing in 1928 John Adams, a Professor of Education at London University, gives a telling explanation of why educational theory took this somewhat uncritical form:

> When education as such began to be recognized...as a subject in University curricula, it was only natural that lectures in education should look out through world literature for great names wherewith to adorn their list of prescribed readings. Quite naturally, Socrates, Plato and Aristotle were seized on at the very start and a good deal of ingenuity was shown in bringing out educational principles from their work....Even at the present day, the best way for a young lecturer in education to establish his claim as an educationalist is to select some well known writer and publish a book under the title 'so and so as Educator'.

Needless to say, this kind of 'Great educators'

approach to educational theory was immediately perceived to be inadequate to the actual needs of teachers and schools-needs that were then being shaped by the expansion in state education resulting from the Forster Education Act of 1876 and the Balfour Education Act of 1902. Although it was always intended that this expansion would give expression to a variety of educational aspirations and ideals, it was also firmly linked to an overriding pragmatic concern: the need to create a highly differentiated labour force equipped to fill the range of occupational roles appropriate to the advancement of a model industrial society. This, in turn, meant that education had to be institutionalized to an unprecedented degree, not only to ensure that educational provision and the flow of qualified teachers could be regulated and controlled, but also to make sure that the policies of schools, the content of their curriculum, and their methods of assessment were more securely harnessed to the economic needs of society.

One of the major effects of this new level of institutionalization was gradually to transform the way in which education itself was understood. It now became increasingly attractive to see education as a 'system' which had to be efficiently organized, managed, and administered. Moreover, a necessary prerequisite for the effective management and administration of this 'system' was the creation of a greater consensus about the goals of education. And the need to make education more responsive to economic demands made it imperative that this consensus took it as self-evident that a primary goal of education was to prepare pupils for the kind of occupational positions available in modern society.

In this climate of increasingly institutionalized educational provision, educational theory had to develop new forms. The most pressing problems were not how philosophical problems about the purpose of education, but instrumental problems about how education was to achieve those social and economic purposes prescribed in modern society. What was needed was a form of educational theorizing which could suggest better ways of achieving accepted and established educational goals rather than simply provoking a seemingly endless dialogue about what these goals should be. The form of educational theory which emerged to fill this need was one which construed educational theory as an 'applied science'-a form of theorizing designed to produce a body of sophisticated scientific principles and techniques which could be used to improve the functioning of the educational system.

One of the earliest and clearest examples of the link between this 'applied science' approach to educational theory and the demand being made of educational practice is the emergence of psychometry in the 1920s. Under the powerful leadership of Sir Cyril Birt, a 'scientific' theory of human intelligence was invoked in order to legitimize procedures for measuring the 'educability' of pupils-procedures that were urgently required if schools were effectively to segregate pupils in line with the demand for a hierarchical and stratified division of labour. The interconnections that obtained throughout the interwar period between educational theorizing of a predominantly psychometric kind and the rise of mass education have often been discussed by educational historians. Brian Simon, for example, has made it clear that any explanation of why psychometry dominated educational theory throughout this period.

Actual circumstances of the time which called insistently for theories which legitimised the hierarchical system brought into being from 1902. There appears to be a clear relationship between the economic and social conditions..in the interwar period...and the dominant theory legitimising and lubricating this system

In the period immediately following the second world war, educational theories of an applied science form proliferated and affected all area of educational practice. Behaviourist theories of teaching and learning, bureaucratic approaches to educational organization, and administration and technical models of curriculum development appeared-all purporting to improve education by applying scientific principles and knowledge. By the early 1950s educational theory had become fully accommodated to the scientific and technological spirit of the age. Fundamental philosophical questions about the purpose of education and its relationship to society could no longer find adequate theoretical expression, and educational theory surrendered its traditional claims to offer moral guidance and support. As educational practice was transformed into a neutral instrument for pursuing given social objectives, so educational theory was transformed into a neutral instrument for overcoming the technical problems to which the pursuit of these objectives gave rise.

By the 1960s other academic disciplines had joined psychology in making claims to have important applications to educational practice. Sociology had become an established empirical science, providing research findings critical of existing selection procedures and supportive of egalitarian proposals to extend equality of opportunity through comprehensive reorganization.

Educational philosophy resurfaced with a new name-the philosophy of education'-but in a truncated and much reduced form. Drawing inspiration from the 'linguistic revolution' that had already transformed mainstream academic philosophy, the new 'philosophy of education' was no longer defined by the enduring nature of the questions it addressed but by the particular methods it employed-a method of 'conceptual analysis' by means of which the 'logic' of the concepts used in everyday educational discourse could be 'clarified'. By embracing this method the philosophy of education could claim that it was no longer contaminated by rival 'educational ideologies', but had now followed other forms of educational theory in becoming a respectable value-neutral academic pursuit.

Throughout the 1960s, as educational theory became increasingly dependent on the 'parent' disciplines of philosophy, psychology, and sociology, so it was increasingly seen to rest on foundations that were outside the field of education itself. It is hardly surprising, therefore, that the officially sanctioned view that dominated this period defined educational theory as a stock of 'practical principles' that were entirely justified by appeal to knowledge provided by the 'foundation' disciplines. At a theoretical level, this inter-disciplinary' view of educational theory derived its main impetus from the collection of papers in J.W. Tibble's The Study of Education. At an organizational level, the philosophy, psychology and sociology 'of education' had, by the end of the 1960s, managed to carve up the domain of educational theory amongst themselves. Educational departments were reorganized, courses in educational studies were restructured, professional identities were changed, and new journals and academic societies were established, all displaying total allegiance to the view that educational theory was nothing other than the application to education of these 'foundation' disciplines. By 1970, educational theory as an autonomous field of practical knowledge had ceased to exist.

Almost immediately, however, the initial enthusiasm for this kind of educational theory was tempered by a growing realization that the 'educational disciplines' did not easily relate to educational practice. Practical educational problems were not accessible from the narrow confines of the academic disciplines, and the interdisciplinary co-operation between philosophers, psychologists, and sociologists which this approach envisaged never actually got off the ground. As it became clear that 'academic respectability' had only been achieved at the price of 'practical relevance', so complaints about 'the disciplines approach' intensified. As a result, the past decade has been marked by attempts to forge a new 'paradigm' which would bridge the 'gaps' between educational theory and the educational practice to which it s supposedly addressed.

One of the most influential of these new paradigms has emerged in the field of curriculum theory, where reactions against the increasing use of scientific and technical language have been particularly strong. This overreliance of curriculum theory on academic and scientific theories was explicitly recognized and attacked by Joseph Schwab in his seminal paper, The practical: a language for the curriculum. In this, Schwab mounts a critique which is equally telling against both the 'applied science' and the 'disciplines' view of educational theory. Briefly, what he argues is that: these approaches fragment the curriculum as an object of study; distort education as a mode of autonomous practice; fail to equip teachers to make informed practical judgements; lead to contradiction and confusion, and foreclose discussion about the moral aspects of education and its role in modern society. Schwab thus proposes a view of curriculum theorizing as a 'practical' discipline. He makes it clear, that

> By the 'practical' I do not mean the curbstone practicality of the mediocre administrator and the man on the street for whom the practical means the easily achieved familiar goals which can be reached by familiar means. I refer rather to a complex discipline relatively unfamiliar to the academic and differing radically from the disciplines of the theoretic. It is the discipline concerned with choice and action, in contrast with the theoretic. It is the discipline concerned with choice and action, in contrast with the theoretic, which is concerned with knowledge. Its methods lead to defensible decisions where the methods of the theoretic lead to warranted conclusions.

When Schwab's 'practical' approach erupted onto the American scene, it quickly attracted adherents from the ranks of those curriculum theorists who were disaffected by the dominant technical and theoretical perspective. In Britain, the main focus for this kind of unrest was provided by Lawrence Stenhouse's influential vision of curriculum theorizing as a form of creative and critical inquiry through which teachers could explicitly explore their own implicit educational 'theories' by researching their own educational practice. This gave rise to a radically new understanding of 'educational theory'-one which asserted the indivisibility of theory and practice and which gave the notion of 'teacher-as-researcher; a central place.

As developed by Schwab, Stenhouse, and others, 'practical' approaches to educational theorizing have now emerged which reinstate the image of the teacher as a professional educator whose deliberations about what to teach and how to teach it are once again informed by philosophical beliefs and ethical concerns. At the same time, however, it is apparent that the progressive institutionalization of education has severely curtailed the extent to which teachers are still able to construe their work as an ethical activity based on morally informed deliberation and choice. As a result, many educational theorists are becoming more conscious of the need to expose the ways in which the institutionalized mechanisms that now regulate the work of schools may be frustrating teachers in their attempts to express their professional aspirations and pursue genuine educational values and goals.

The anti-educational effect of the institutionalization of schooling was itself made a major topic of debate by the de-schooling polemic of the 1970s. Ivan Illich, the chief architect and principal exponent of de-schooling argued that because schools had, in effect, become social institutions serving the economic needs of modern technological society, they could not longer operate as viable educational communities serving the learning and developmental needs of their individual pupils. This argument not only challenged the cherished belief that more schooling equals more education; it also challenged educational theorists to develop a form of educational theorizing which did not simply solve the technical problems arising within the institutionalized educational system, but raised critical questions about how the process of institutionalization had itself become a major obstacle to genuine educational development and reform.

This challenge is now being met by the development of a new 'paradigm' of educational theory-a critical paradigm-which, like philosophical and practical forms of educational theorizing, incorporates a central concern with fundamental questions about the nature of education and its role in society. What makes it distinctive is that it is also concerned to explore the social, political and economic structures within which educational provision and practice are now embedded. It is thus a form of theorizing specifically designed to raise critical questions about the tensions and contradictions that occur between prevailing social values and educational values. In particular it seeks to reveal how the process of institutionalization may distort educational values and constrain opportunities for their practical realization.

Once it is considered from a historical perspective, it is clear that the evolution of educational theory is not one of progressive development towards a unified interpretation of its meaning and use. On the contrary, the history of educational theory is the history of an ever-increasing range of different interpretation each of which has merged in response to a changing political climate and a changing agenda of practical concerns. What this suggests is that any quest for a unitary view of 'educational theory' is illusory. What it also suggests is that the diverse range of approaches to educational theory that has emerged during the last hundred years or so is not simply the product of an on-going 'philosophical' debate about the kind of 'theory' appropriate for education to adopt. It is also the product of an on-going political debate about educational policy and practice. This connection between interpretations of educational theory and interpretations of educational practice is usually left implicit and undisclosed. In order to make it more explicit and visible, it may now be useful to summarize the major forms of educational theorizing that have emerged in the twentieth century in a way that draws attention to the rival views of educational practice each incorporates.

The common-sense approach

This approach is favoured by many members of the teaching profession and the HMI. As the name indicates, it refers to those approaches which base educational theory on a common-sense understanding of practice. Thus, with this approach educational theory is always 'practice-focused'; educational theorizing is simply a matter of codifying ideas, concepts and principles embedded in practice and then using this 'theory' to test practical competence and identify deficiencies in practical performance. With this kinds of theory, fundamental value-laden questions about educational practice are regarded as uncontentious and largely ignored. Practice determines theory rather than theory determining practice. Educational practice is on this view, simply a mater of acting within a given tradition.

The philosophical approach

Within this approach 'common sense' is regarded as to unreflective and uncritical to provide an adequate basis for educational theory, it therefore offers a form of theorizing designed to enable practitioners to extend and enrich their common-sense thinking by relating it to a philosophical understanding of the true meaning and purpose of education. Educational practice, therefore, is no interpreted simply as a form of common-sense action but as a form of reflective practice based on educational ideals which can be articulated and justified in the light of some coherent 'philosophy'.

The 'applied science' approach

This is the approach adopted by those educational psychologist, educational researchers, and curriculum evaluators who insist that any defensible view of educational theory must conform to standards laid down by science. On this view, educational theory is a form of 'applied science', using value-free empirical knowledge as a basis for resolving educational problems and improving educational practice. Because, in this approach, questions about the 'ends' of education involve value judgements which cannot be settled scientifically, they cannot therefore be a legitimate concern of educational theory. The only genuinely scientific questions that educational theory can resolve are instrumental questions about the most effective means of achieving those educational ends that have been deemed desirable. Because if incorporated this view of education as a means to a given end, the applied science approach always interprets educational practice as a technical activity: a neutral instrument for bringing about some 'given' educational goals.

The 'practical' approach

This is the approach underpinning 'illuminative' and 'naturalistic' approaches to curriculum evaluation and research and 'process' models of curriculum development. With this approach, the aim of educational theory is not to provide solutions to technical problems but to help practitioners to make morally defensible judgements. It seeks to do this by rehabilitating the practical art of 'deliberation' as a basis for acting educationally in particular practical situations. Thus, from this perspective, educational practice is morally informed action; it is an essentially ethical activity guided by educational values rather than any narrow utilitarian concerns. 'Practice' is thus not seen as an instrumental means to some fixed educational end s but as a fluid and flexible activity in which the choice of both means and ends is guided by values immanent in the educational process itself.

The critical approach

Although this approach has yet to penetrate fully the field of education, it is now the subject of considerable discussion and debate. Like the 'practical' approach, this approach rejects the view of educational theory as an 'applied science' and sees it instead as a form of 'moral science' in which the importance of educational aims and values is given full recognition. Where it differs from the 'practical' view is in its explicit recognition of how practitioners' own understanding of their educational aims may become distorted by various non-educational social forces and of how the practical realization of their values may be impeded by institutional structures and political constraints. Educational practice is thus interpreted not simply as a moral practice but also as a social practice which is historically located, culturally embedded, and hence always shaped by ideology.

In education today, these rival views of theory and practice compete with one another for the allegiance of theorists, researchers, policy makers, and teachers. Those who view educational practice as a form of activity based on inherited tradition and common sense will favour the approach to educational theory which endorses this view

Those who see educational practice as an essentially instrumental activity-as a means to some uncontentious fixed ends-want a form of theorizing which can produce solutions to the technical problems to which attempts to achieve those ends give rise. Others, because they see educational practice as primarily a moral activity, are attracted to a form of theorizing in which the ethical quality of the professional judgements of practitioners is given a central place. Yet others, for whom the ethical dimension of educational practice is being gradually subverted by the modern institutionalization of education, support a form of educational theorizing that can expose the contradictions between educational values and institutionally imposed values, bring them under critical scrutiny, and make them more open to rational dialogue and debate.

Normally, the interdependence of these competing views of theory and practice is either unacknowledged or undisclosed. Indeed, it is common for both educational theorists and practitioners to regard methodological debates about the nature and purpose of educational theory as quite separate from political debates about the nature and purpose of educational practice. What I have tried to show in this paper is that they are not. In education, theory is an indispensable dimension of practice.

Index